# THE
# GARMENT OF GOD

## by
## David Jones

The Garment of God

All scripture references are taken from the NIV version of the Bible,
unless otherwise noted. Copyright © 1973, 1978 International Bible
Society. Published by Hodder and Stoughton

ISBN 978-0-9957386-1-4

Published by Royston Bethel Community Church, Bride Ministries

Book designed & formatted by Laura Murray at Peanut Designs
www.pnutd.co.uk

# Dedicated to

Joseph, Libby, Jemima and Isaac,
who I pray will wear the garment of God.

# The Garment of God

'We groan, longing to be clothed'

'Clothe yourself in the Lord Jesus Christ.'

**~ Paul**


'Clothe yourself with strength! Put on your garments of splendour'

'He has clothed me with garments of salvation and arrayed me in a robe of righteousness.'

**~ Isaiah**


'He is dressed in a robe dipped in blood…the armies of heaven were following him, dressed in fine linen, white and clean.'

**~ John**


'Be dressed ready for service.'

'They will walk with me dressed in white, for they are worthy.'

**~ Jesus**

# Contents

# Introduction

*'The LORD wraps himself in light as with a garment.'*

*Psalm 104:2*

$G$od clothes everything. All things in his creation have a specific covering that has been specially manufactured as a garment to be worn. Mammals are clothed in fur, fish are covered in scales and birds are coated in feathers. Their coverings were woven into the fabric of their physical bodies at the beginning of their creation on earth. Even in heaven angelic beings are robed in clothes as white as snow[1], but when God created man, he wore no garment; man was created naked.

The question arises as to why God made the decision not to provide clothes for Adam and Eve at their creation. In order to answer and understand this question, it must be grasped that God had indeed provided a garment for

---

1        Matt. 27:3

the rulers of his creation to wear. From the beginning, the Holy Trinity had planned that mankind would wear a special and specific item of clothing. It would be unlike anything else worn in the whole of God's creation and was only to adorn those made in his own image. In order to fully appreciate the quality and unique nature of this robe, God would write an entire book describing the specific attributes of this special clothing. The prophets would write about it, the psalmist's would sing about it, and the patriarchs would wear it. Every book of the Bible has something to say about the clothing he has created for mankind to wear.

*Isa. 61:10 'He has clothed me with garments of salvation and arrayed me in a robe of righteousness.'*

The Old Testament prophets predicted a day when God would perfectly clothe his people. They described what this garment would look like, who would wear it and even what it would smell like. They illuminated its power and blessing upon those who wore it and warned against the dangers of abusing or neglecting its covering.

> *It would be worn by those who were anointed and favoured by God*

They knew it would be worn by those who were anointed and favoured by God. It would clothe priests and kings, prophets and leaders. Brides and warriors would be wrapped up in its protection and power. It was a heavenly robe - pure, clean, holy and unlike anything of this fallen world. They declared that one day this garment would be ready for God's people to wear and they prophesied the divine nature of this robe.

*Rom. 13:14 'Clothe yourself in the Lord Jesus Christ.'*

The garment was fully displayed when the Messiah finally arrived. When Jesus walked the land of Israel he gave the perfect demonstration of what it was to be clothed in the Holy Spirit of God. Everything he did, and even the clothes he wore, were a prophetic sign that pointed to what God had provided. From the strips of cloth at his birth[2] to the seamless robe at his death[3], people recognised that his clothing had prophetic significance to all of mankind. Even as he was about to ascend into heaven he instructed his disciples to wait for the clothing he was going to send them.[4]

Now that Christ is glorified, that clothing is now available to all men. This robe is a picture of all the fullness that has been provided by God the Father, the Son, and the Holy Spirit. It encapsulates all that the Trinity

---

2        Luke 2:12
3        John 19:23
4        Luke 24:49

desires for the life of every believer. The story of God's clothing is a perfect metaphor for all who desire to live under, and be covered by, the Holy Spirit. This is the story of the Garment of God.

# 1

## Man's Nakedness

*'They realised they were naked.'*

**Gen. 3:7**

*T*he first thing that Adam and Eve realised after they had sinned against God was that they were naked. No one had to tell them. They knew in their innermost being that there was now a defect within their nature and it had to be covered up. Man's sinful nakedness needed to be clothed. Just as God cannot look upon sin, he has also said that he rejects the consequences of disobedience. The naked bodies of fallen humanity would have to be adequately covered before they were again acceptable to God. The fear of this nakedness being exposed terrified Adam and Eve and it still haunts the minds of all their children today. Everyone is born naked into this world and the Bible is full of stories addressing man's problem of being correctly clothed in the sight of God. Thousands of years after Eden, in another garden, one of Jesus' own disciples ran away from his master rather than have his nakedness exposed.[5] Today, many run from the presence of God in a similar way, rather than accepting that their clothing has been lost. Others hide away like Adam amongst the trees. Sadly, everyone tries to manufacture their own clothing, despite the obvious futility of this endeavour.

*Gen. 3:7 'so they sewed fig leaves together and made coverings for themselves.'*

The first activity Adam and Eve embarked on was making garments for themselves. They falsely presumed that the consequences of their sin could be covered up by wearing clothes that their own hands had made. They reasoned, because their sin had been caused by eating the fruit of a forbidden tree, their clothing should be made from the leaves of an acceptable tree. They failed to grasp that just as eating the fruit came from their own disobedience, so the self-manufacture of the leaves would, likewise, be rejected as unacceptable clothing. God will never accept the garments of fallen man's hands as they are filthy rags in his sight.[6]

---

5        Mark 14
6        Isa. 64:6

*Gen. 3:21 'The LORD God made garments of skin for Adam and his wife and clothed them.'*

Despite man's sin and his fear of being naked, God had already embarked upon a plan to save him. He would undertake in his situation and through his divine foreknowledge, provide a covering for Adam. He would make a garment for them to wear. Instead of fig leaves, they would be clothed with the garment from God. It would be no ordinary piece of clothing, but would have very specific attributes. This garment would be a covering that belonged to another lifeform before it was given to man.

*This garment would be a covering that belonged to another lifeform before it was given to man.*

This other being would have to die so that Adam's nakedness could be clothed. The covering given to Adam would have to be a garment that was powerful enough to cover Adam's sin and so pure that it would be acceptable to the eyes of God.

An innocent animal would be sacrificed in order for Adam to be acceptably clothed. Every acceptable sacrificial animal in the Bible is merely a picture of the eternal sacrifice that made atonement for man's sin. It is a picture of Jesus Christ, who was the Lamb slain from the foundation of the world.[7] He was the sheep who would be sheared, and the lamb who would be slaughtered,[8] so that mankind could be clothed.

*Matt. 27:28 'They stripped Him.'*

*John 19:23 'They took His clothes, dividing them into four shares, one for each of them, with the undergarment remaining.'*

For man's nakedness to be covered, the acceptable sacrifice had to be stripped of its own clothing. Christ's blood had to be shed to atone for man's sin, but Jesus also had to be stripped in order for man to wear his garment. Not only did Jesus surrender his outer clothing, but all his garments had to be removed. Even the very skin on his body was flayed away by a brutal lashing from a Roman whip. He was skinned alive, so that man could be clothed. He wilfully gave away all he had to cover the nakedness of the people that He loved. Even the cruel legionaries who tortured and flogged him, were given the privilege of wearing his clothes. The same soldier who nailed him to a tree, went home wearing his linen garment that very day.

The same opportunity is available for every person alive today. Despite their sins, God's love has purchased a garment to cover their nakedness.

---

7        Rev. 13:8
8        Isa. 53:7

They don't deserve it any more than the Roman soldier at Calvary. Nevertheless God has supplied the perfect sacrifice to provide all the children of Adam with acceptable clothing. Everyone who accepts Jesus as their atoning sacrifice, can also be clothed in his righteousness.[9]

## *Satan's Plan*

*Gen 9:22 'Ham, the father of Canaan, saw his father naked and told his two brothers outside.'*

Satan's plan has always been to blind mankind to God's loving provision and to continually expose man's sin and nakedness. Satan's children follow his same tactics. Ham chose to gossip about his father's sin, whilst his brothers would ensure that it was covered. Instead of trying to help cover someone's nakedness, evil people would rather expose it. Good people believe that a covering has been provided.

The Devil's children are experts at pointing out the nakedness of those around them, and they scrutinise every tiny detail of a person's life in order to uncover the slightest fault. Once found, they delight to bring accusation and point out every fault in the hope of causing extreme embarrassment and acute fear. They hope to drive everyone into hiding and away from receiving God's loving provision of a covering garment.

---

9        Isa. 61:10

Satan's threats and intimidation can cause crushing anxiety to people, with the aim that exposing someone's nakedness will cause continual pain. Just like David's servants hiding in embarrassment at Jericho when an evil ruler cut away their garments, many also hide their nakedness from the presence of their king.[10]

People still hide from God when wicked people threaten to expose their faults. Satan can even direct and use demonic spirits to cause nakedness, as when a demon possessed man stripped the sons of Sceva, leaving them naked and bleeding.[11] Despite being religious and using all the correct spiritual words, Sceva's sons ended up being just as naked as Adam in Eden. Satan's demons are not afraid of man's religion or spiritual efforts; they are only afraid of Jesus.


*Luke 8:27 'Jesus was met by a demon possessed man from the town. For a long time this man had not worn clothes.'*

Like the man attacked in Jesus' parable of the Good Samaritan, Satan's lies leave people afraid, beaten up and naked.[12] Once Evil has control of a person's mind, he can exploit their fears and abuse their nakedness. Despite his tactics, everyone can find hope when coming to Jesus.

---

10      1 Chron. 19:4-5
11      Acts 19:16
12      Luke 10:30

Whatever anyone's condition, God's plan has always been to provide everyone with his garment. When this tormented man met Jesus, his life was changed forever. Not only was the evil removed from his life and his sanity restored; Jesus made sure that the man was also clothed. The people of the local town heard about the man's deliverance and 'When they came to Jesus they found the man from whom the demons had gone out, sitting at Jesus' feet, DRESSED.'[13] Jesus' aim was to provide the man with garments, as well as deliver him from evil. When God saves a man, he also clothes him.


*Mat 6:28 'Why do you worry about clothes?*

*Luke 12:28 'If God clothes the grass of the field...how much more will he cloth you, O you of little faith.'*

Jesus instructed his children that they should never worry about being left naked. The Heavenly Father always provides the appropriate clothing for his children. Christians must not give way to fear, thinking that their nakedness has been overlooked by God. Christ not only purchased forgiveness of sins, he provided garments of righteousness for his followers to wear. Man's nakedness has been fully addressed by God's gracious gift. All true Christians long to wear God's garment 'because

---

13      Luke 8:35

when we are clothed, we will not be found naked.'[14] Jesus was very clear that failure to grasp the provision of his clothing was due to unbelief, and that absence of faith is a sign of sin.[15] Adequate clothing is provided when true faith is present, but fear of nakedness in a child of God is evidence of unbelief. Christ's church must never be naked.

## *The Naked Church*

*Rev. 3:17 'you do not realise that you are naked.'*

Although Adam and Eve recognised their nakedness immediately, the church in Laodicea was totally unaware that it wore no garment. The churches that had the biggest problems in the book of Revelation were also the same ones that were rebuked for not understanding the state of their clothing.[16] Despite thousands of years of Biblical understanding, God's own church had still refused to wear the clothes that he had prepared for it. Instead of being clothed with Christ's glory, the Laodiceans were still naked. This church was so self-satisfied with its own wealth and achievements, it saw no need to wear the garment of God. The Christians at Laodicea were so full of pride that they had become blind to their real condition of nakedness before God. What is so lamentable, is that they

---

14      2 Cor. 5:3
15      Rom. 14:23
16      Rev. 3:4

did not even appear to be listening to Christ's call for them to get dressed. What was true of the final church in John's vision, is a direct parallel to the state of the church at the closing of the present age. It reveals a group of believers who are preoccupied with their own selfish concerns and in accumulating material possessions. Unfortunately, many in the western church are unaware of their naked state just like those in Laodicea.

*Song of Songs 5:3 'I have taken off my robe – must I put it on again?'*
When a person first comes to know the Lord, they are well aware of their nakedness without him. They recognise their need to repent from sin and put their faith in Jesus Christ. Sadly, after a season, many Christians allow their love to become cold towards God and forget that the garment of salvation has to be worn at all times. Spiritual laziness can deceive a believer into thinking that Christ's robe can be kept in a closet until Sunday, rather than understanding that it must be worn continually. Just because someone has received grace to become a Christian does not mean that they can abuse that grace and allow themselves to become unclothed. Attending church does not, necessarily, mean that a Christian is clothed. Jesus proved this by writing to his own church saying, 'I counsel you to buy…white clothes to wear, so you can cover your

shameful nakedness.[17]' This instruction from the Lord was given to the last church in the list. It is interesting to note that it is probably the last church of the age that has the greatest danger of becoming unclothed. It is the church of today - especially the rich, western Christians - who are most at risk of discarding their garments due to their false sense of prosperity and security. Worldly wealth can become a great danger to a believer, leading them into spiritual lethargy and selfish contentment. Every Christian must heed the words of Jesus and ensure that they are wearing the garment he has provided. Nakedness will never be accepted by God. He has provided the garments and he expects them to be worn at all times.

*Rev 16:15 'Behold, I come as a thief! Blessed is he who stays awake and keeps his clothes with him, so that he may not go naked and be shamefully exposed.'*

Being unclothed is not optional for a believer; God's garment is a necessity. For a Christian to be found naked, is the greatest shame. It means they have rejected the very Lord and saviour to whom they claim to belong. Failure to get dressed will result in increased problems for God's people. The woman in the Song of Songs went through tribulation

---

17        Rev. 3:18

because she failed to get dressed for her beloved. She confessed that her tormentors found her and 'they beat me, they bruised me; they took away my cloak.'[18] It is worthy of note, that failure to get dressed when she was called resulted in her cloak being taken away at a later date. It is very sobering for the church to realise that failing to wear the garment that God has given to us may result in us losing it altogether. This is a risk too great to take, but, unfortunately, history has shown that many people who have once been clothed have later discarded their garment.

## Permanent Nakedness?

*Ezek. 16:8 'I spread the corner of my garment over you and covered your nakedness'*

The prophet Ezekiel tells the story of God's people being chosen and clothed with his garment. He lavished expensive clothes upon the people and called them his special possession. Unfortunately, the very people who once wore God's garment would later be stripped bare and left naked.[19] It needs to be understood by all who belong to God, that it is the greatest privilege to wear His clothing. By his immeasurable grace, God gave us Christ's garment of righteousness. Without it we are left naked in

---

18      Song of Songs 5:7
19      Ezek. 16:39

carnality and sin. Ezekiel describes how someone can lose their garment, and it begins when 'you did not remember the days of your youth, when you were naked and bare.'[20] When people forget that they were naked without God, they can begin to devalue the clothing that he has provided for them. Once this occurs, their relationship with Christ deteriorates resulting in continual nakedness. The result of this rejection of God's essential covering runs the risk of becoming permanent nakedness. In the light of all that God has provided, there can surely be no greater loss than to be eternally naked and banished from his presence.

---

20       Ezek. 16:22

# 2

# Garment of Favour

*'The Father said to his servants, Quick! Bring the best Robe and put it on him.'*

***Luke 15:22***

Since Adam became naked and left God's presence, the Father has longed for the day when His children will return. He knows that without his garment they will remain in a wretched condition. When a lost son returns to his father's house, there is a garment waiting for him to wear. In the story of the prodigal son, God has revealed to everyone the true nature of his heart, which is that He longs to clothe them in his best robe. Whenever people leave their sin and return to God in true repentance, they do not just become clothed with any ordinary garment; they wear the finest robe that God has available, the clothes of his most beloved son, with whom he is well pleased.[21] The same covering that God had for Jesus is now available to all his children and he desires that they wear the garment of favour.

---

21      Luke 3:22

### Clothes of the First-born

*Gen. 27:15 'Rebekah took the best clothes of Esau, her older son...and put them on her younger son Jacob.'*

Jacob could never receive the father's blessing by wearing his old clothes. He had to gain access to the garment of the first-born. It was the first-born son who received the inheritance and it was the older brother who would receive the greatest blessing. The first-born son received the most favour from the father because he was loved above all others,[22] and Jacob knew this. Today this principle still holds true. Jesus is the only begotten firstborn son of God and all the favour of the Father is placed upon him. It is important to note that when the full blessing of God was pronounced upon Jesus on the mount of transfiguration, the glory of this favour was displayed through his clothing.[23] For anyone to receive and experience this divine favour, they must also wear the garments of the first-born son of God. Jesus is the elder brother of all who believe and he has made his robes available to all, so that they may receive the blessing of his father and

> *The glory of this favour was displayed through his clothing.*

---

22      Gen. 25:28
23      Matt. 17:5

share in his inheritance. Just as the King's first born son Jonathan gave his clothes to David, Jesus gives His garments to Christians in order for them to be appropriately dressed in the King's presence.[24]

*Gen. 27:16 'She also covered his hands and neck with goat skins.'*

Before Jacob could wear the garments of the first-born, a sacrifice had to be made. Just as Adam was clothed in the skins from an acceptable sacrifice, so Jacob was clothed in the fleece of a slaughtered animal from the flock. Before anyone can wear the garment of favour, they must submit to the reality of the only true life that God accepts. It is only through the 'Lamb who was slain'[25] that anyone can be accepted by God. Only Jesus is 'The Lamb who takes away the sin of the world.'[26] Too many people are in such a hurry to wear the garment of favour that they have overlooked the sacrifice that was necessary to obtain it. Once the gravity of that sacrifice has been understood, the garment is able to be worn. Whatever it takes, everyone must seize the opportunity to be clothed in order to obtain the father's blessing. Genuine faith will stop at nothing in order to be found in Christ.[27]

---

24      1 Sam. 18:4
25      Rev. 5:12
26      John 1:29
27      Phil. 3:9

*Gen. 27:27 'When Isaac caught the smell of his clothes, he blessed him.'*

It was the garment of the beloved son that brought the blessing and not Jacob's own efforts. Jacob did not deserve anything, but the clothes that he wore guaranteed favour from the father. When Isaac smelled the clothes, his blessing was dispensed. God's favour on any life depends on whose clothes they are wearing. It is the aroma that God recognises. When Noah offered an acceptable sacrifice, 'The LORD smelled the pleasing aroma'[28] and blessed his family. God's favour will not dwell with a bad smell. It is the fragrance of Christ that pleases the nostrils of God, not man's own works. It is only of Christ that the Psalmist said, 'All your robes are fragrant with myrrh and aloes and cassia.'[29] Christians must wear Christ's robes if they want to smell like Jesus. When they wear the garment of God's favour they 'are to God the pleasing aroma of Christ.'[30]

### Joseph's Garment

*Gen. 37:3 'Israel loved Joseph more than any of his other sons...and he made a richly ornamented robe for him.'*

God's love for his favoured children is never hidden. It is lavished upon them.[31] The grace and favour that Jacob gave to Joseph was displayed

---

28      Gen. 8:21
29      Psalm 45:8
30      2 Cor. 2:15
31      1 John 3:1

in the garment that he gave him to wear. Jacob knew that it was through wearing the favoured garment that he had obtained blessing in his own life and he would ensure that his most beloved son would also wear the favoured robe. The garment that you wear reveals who you are in the eyes of God. Unfortunately, Satan also sees the garment that God has given to you and he hates it. He despises everything that it represents and detests the fact that anyone is loved by God. He will stop at nothing to take it from every child of God and plans to strip them of all that Christ has given them. Joseph's life reveals an example of the correct way to remain under God's blessing, despite the devil's attack to strip him of his robe.

*Gen. 37:23 'When Joseph came to his brothers, they stripped him of his robe – the richly ornamented robe he was wearing.'*

Beware the older brothers. Creation's first older brother was also the first murderer.[32] It was the older brother who hated that the fathers garment had been given to the prodigal son.[33] It was the older brother who planned to kill Jacob when he wore the clothes of blessing[34] and it was the older brothers who would strip Joseph of the father's robe. When a Christian

---

32        Gen. 4:8
33        Luke 15:28
34        Gen. 27:41

receives the garment of God they may falsely assume that most people would be pleased for them. They can often assume that now they have left their nakedness of sin and have come to be clothed in God's favour, other people will think better of them. Sadly, the opposite is usually true. Instead of being happy with the favour and gifting that Joseph's robe designated, his brothers hated him with murderous intent. They were jealous of his status and could not bear to look at his beautiful robe. Joseph's garment reminded them of their failures, and his talent's and gifting only called attention to their own lack of faith. When God bestows gifting to his children, others who are bereft of true love and faith may hate them. Anyone called to a favoured position in God's household must recognise the disdain that some older brothers will have for them if they insist on wearing God's robe. To wear the garment of God will please the father but will incite hatred amongst the ungodly older brethren. Their hatred began with having a bitter attitude toward their brother, but developed into actual harm being enacted upon Joseph and the robe he wore. Many ministers have to endure similar bitterness from other brothers when God gives them divine favour. They may endure character assassinations from people they trusted, and can painfully observe the public ripping-apart of their ministries. God's favour, however, can never be removed by the jealous hatred of other people.

*Gen. 39:12 'She caught him by his cloak and said "come to bed with me!" But he left his cloak in her hand and ran out of the house.'*

Despite having his ornamented robe torn apart by his brothers, Joseph continued to trust God and prospered as the leading servant in Potiphar's house. Although he still enjoyed God's favour, he now wore a different garment; one of service. For a Christian to enjoy God's favour they must also embrace the willingness to serve. The mantle that is placed upon God's children is not for mere decoration, but practical ministry.

Joseph worked hard and was soon applauded by everyone for his abilities and diligence. There was, however, another problem in his life that was associated with his clothing. His garments now attracted inappropriate desire, instead of hatred. Potiphar's wife did not hate Joseph's clothes, but instead wanted to possess them for herself. This type of misappropriation of the garment of favour will produce equally disastrous results.

Many Christians can pass the test of having their robes hated by jealous brothers, but seem unaware of other dangers and temptations associated with their garments of favour. Some people can eye a person's garments with selfish desire. They can see that certain individuals possess powerful gifts and have great favour from God, so can seek to use and manipulate these for themselves. Like Potiphar's wife, they can view God's ministers as a way of satisfying their own lusts. They may assume that God's servants are there to keep their carnal desires satisfied. Such people may use flattery and seduction to deceive ministers into thinking they can take advantage of forbidden things. Once ensnared, these ministers may believe their special abilities make them invulnerable to temptation, or that they are above it.

Joseph took wise action when his garment was grabbed by an unclean temptation: he fled from it.


*Gen. 39:18 'As soon as I screamed for help, he left his cloak beside me and ran out of the house.'*

When someone wears the garment of favour, other people will spread lies about them. If not given what they crave, they will use the clothing worn by God's servant against him. Joseph's robe was used in false accusation to imprison him. If he had never used his abilities to serve the house in the first place, he would not have been subject to accusation and condemnation. Jesus said that wearing his garment means that some will falsely accuse you and say all kinds of evil against you[35] because you

---

35      Matt. 5:11

belong to Christ. Let such liars take what they will. God's favour will never be removed from those he has genuinely chosen. Christ himself had his garments taken from him while being accused and spat at.[36] But the lies of men would not change who he was. Evildoers may strip people of their robes, but God always re-clothes his children with his divine favour.

*Gen. 41:41 'Pharaoh took his signet ring from his finger and put it on Joseph's finger. He dressed him in robes of fine linen.'*

Despite years of unjust suffering in prison, Joseph's favour had not been removed. God was still with him, and, as he continued to have faith in God, the day came when he lost his prison clothes and wore the finest garment of his life. The king himself robed Joseph in fine linen. What God has given his children, no man can take away. God's favour always results in his garments being placed upon his children. They never have to manufacture their own success. Joseph would save a nation because he continued to wear the robes that God's providence had placed upon him. Joseph worked for the benefit of others and never clothed himself at any stage of his life.

Not only would he rescue the people of Egypt, he would also become the

---

36      Mark 25:29

saviour of his own people. When they were finally reconciled, Joseph would provide each of his brothers with new clothing.[37] Not only were they forgiven of their crime of stripping Joseph, but through his grace he would clothe them with new garments. In the same way, Jesus now provides the garment of favour to all who are reconciled to God. Although it was man's sin that stripped him at the cross, he has forgiven everyone and now they can wear his garment of favour.

.

37      Gen. 45:22

# 3

## Torn Garment

*'When the soldiers crucified Jesus, they took his clothes, dividing them*
*into four shares, one for each of them.'*
### John 19:23

*J*esus was the beloved Son with whom God was well pleased, and he was clothed in the Holy Spirit.[38] Despite wearing the garment of God's favour, sinful man would seek to tear apart these clothes. As has been seen in the story of Joseph, wicked men will tear what the Father gives you to wear. This world hates the garment of God and continually seeks to rip it to pieces. It is disheartening that people seek to tear the spiritual covering of a child of God, but Christ was treated this way, so his followers can expect the same treatment. The soldiers at the cross may not have understood what they were doing, but in tearing Christ's garments they were fulfilling the prophecy of David given a thousand years earlier:

---

38      Luke 3:22

'They divided my garments among them.'[39] Ultimately, God's gifts and calling cannot be taken away from his faithful children, but the Bible has much to say about tearing someone's clothes and it teaches a lesson to all those who will listen.

### *The Torn Garment of the Prophet*

*1 Sam. 15:27-28 'As Samuel turned to leave, Saul caught hold of the hem of his robe and it tore. Samuel said to him, "The LORD has torn the kingdom of Israel from you today."'*

In the Bible, the tearing of a robe was a very symbolic and significant act. It not only brought pain to the wearer, but also signified judgement upon the one who tore it. King Saul had wilfully disobeyed God, which resulted in him being unfit to lead the people. Instead of accepting God's word concerning his leadership, Saul was going to use carnal tactics to hold onto his power. He thought that he could use his abilities of persuasion to coerce other people into obeying his desires. When the prophet Samuel rebuked the king for his pride and disobedience, Saul committed a terrible sin; he tore the robe of the prophet. This rebellious act would result in disaster for the king and his kingdom. The Spirit of God would depart from Saul, despite the fact that he still wore royal robes.

---

39      Psalm 22:18

He would lose his fellowship with the true prophet of God, meaning he would no longer receive divine guidance for success in his battles. Even when he did attempt to contact Samuel at a later date, the spirit of God would strip him of his royal clothes the minute he entered the prophet's presence.[40] When a believer has torn a prophet's garment, they will never be allowed to wear their own. Saul would remember his sinful actions for the rest of his life. Even on the eve of his death when he resorted to divination to obtain a message from Samuel, the witch described the true prophet as a 'man wearing a robe.'[41] On hearing the description of his garment, Saul immediately confessed that it was Samuel. His guilty conscience could not erase the memory of the prophet's robe that he tore.

*Tearing the garment of someone in authority will always result in condemnation from God.*

Tearing the garment of someone in authority will always result in condemnation from God. It has been seen that exposing someone's nakedness will result in a curse, but tearing the garment of a minister whom God has placed over them will result in severe consequences for

---

40      1 Sam. 19:24
41      1 Sam. 28:14

the rebellious person. Today, many Christians follow the example of the world and think that it is acceptable to tear the garments of leaders that they should obey. Instead of listening to guidance and correction from mature pastors, many believers think they know better and insist on having their own way in many matters of life. When such prideful people are rebuked for their disobedience, they often turn upon their leaders, tearing the very prophetic mantles that were given for their own protection. When Joseph's brothers tore apart his robe, they were doing so because they rejected his prophetic dreams that revealed his future leadership of the family. Paul warned the church that it must not 'treat prophesies with contempt,'[42] as this could be the very thing that God is using to protect and lead them.

Of course, this ripping apart of church leadership is rarely a physical action. It is usually done through gossip, misrepresentation, accusation and slander. A Pastor's character is often torn to pieces by people who insist on voicing their own selfish opinions in order to have their own way. Such deluded individuals reject the instruction of scripture to submit to a leader's authority[43] and instead, as Jude describes, use slander and abuse against God's appointed governments. 'These are the very things

---

42        1 Thess. 5:20
43        Heb. 13:17

that destroy them.'[44] Anyone who tears their leader's robes, and fails to repent, will be rejected by God.

### The Torn Garment of the King

*1 Sam. 24:5 'David was conscience stricken for having cut off a corner of his robe.'*

When David tore the garment of his leader, he knew he had committed a grave sin. Despite his closest friends telling him it was God's will to harm Saul (because he deserved it), David knew that tearing the king's robe would bring disaster on his own life. David knew that it was an act for which he must repent, before the severe consequences of such behaviour came to pass. Despite Saul having mistreated David, the man-after-God's-own-heart should not have taken vengeance into his own hands. As God's chosen king, he would indeed wear the garment of God, but not if he tore the robe of his anointed leader. He could not wear a royal garment if he obtained his position by tearing his king's garment. Fortunately, David repented immediately and confessed his error before the consequences of his evil caught up to him.

The avoidance of tearing another person's garment is an essential principle for all Christians to understand. Even when mistreated and

---

44      Jude 1:8-10

falsely accused, a child of God must not react to injustice by ripping another believer's robes. No one can earn the favour of God by tearing blessing from another. Every Christian, when mistreated, should entrust themselves to God (who sees everything), and continue to do good.[45] Even when encouraged to take action by friends, as David was, Christians must not be persuaded that it is acceptable to take such action. The Bible clearly states that the garment of authority must not be torn by man.

*Gen. 37:33-34 'It is my son's robe! ...Then Jacob tore his clothes, put on sackcloth and mourned many days.'*

When Joseph's brothers ripped his garment from him, the consequences of their hatred resulted in the tearing of the clothes of their father, Jacob. The tearing of the robe of one of his sons directly resulted in the garment of the father also being torn. Although the brothers tried to comfort their father, it was to no avail. He had seen the favoured garment of his beloved son ripped apart and that meant his heart was also torn in two.

As well as considering the personal consequences of tearing someone's garment, all believers should seriously contemplate the real pain that will be caused to the heart of God if they do so. God loves his children so much that he clothes them with favour and gifts. He gives them abilities

---

45      1 Pet. 4:19

and ministries according to his omniscient foreknowledge. His grief is real when others think they know better than him and tear away from his children the garments he has clothed them with. The greatest pain to a father's heart is when his children are mistreated and hurt.

*1 Kings 11:30-31 'Ahijah took hold of the new cloak he was wearing and tore it into twelve pieces. Then he said to Jeroboam, "Take ten pieces for yourself."'*

Jeroboam was a talented and gifted leader. He had received great promises from God about his future ministry and had every reason to expect a prosperous future. Unfortunately, when he received a leadership position the power went to his head and his pride led him to disobey God. He would even build a false altar of worship, appoint counterfeit priests and implement idol worship.[46] If he had known what the prophetic symbolism of the torn garment represented, he may have saved himself from destruction. Had he perceived the omen that was present in the prophetic act, he may have understood that God is never pleased with torn leadership and that tearing another's garment on the path to promotion should be avoided at all costs.

God never wants anyone to wear torn robes. Ripped clothes are a sign of

---

46      1 Kings 12:26-33

rejection and curse, never a picture of blessing and prosperity. When a person was discovered to be unclean in the Old Testament, their garments had to be torn as an outward sign of their defilement.[47] When God clothes people in the garments of Christ, they are without defect and are never torn. Jesus instructed his disciples that his new garment of ministry must not be torn.[48] Christians today must not tear people's spiritual clothing. If they do, they must quickly repent or suffer the inevitable consequences of rejection and loss of their own ministry.

## The Torn Garment of the Priest

*Lev. 21:10 'The High Priest...who has been ordained to wear the priestly garments must not tear his clothes.'*

It has been seen that the garment of the prophet and the robes of the king must not be ripped. The Bible is also clear with its command that the garments of God's high priest must never be torn. If the High priest's clothes were ever to be torn, he would die.[49] The robes of priests were specifically designed in such a way as to prevent them from tearing.[50] Everyone anointed to be God's chosen high priest knew that if his clothes were torn he would forfeit his function and ministry. Another priest

47          Lev. 13:45
48          Luke 5:36
49          Lev. 10:6
50          Exd. 28:32

would then be chosen to take his place and the priestly Garments would be placed upon him.

*Mark 14:63 'The High Priest tore his clothes.'*

When Jesus stood before the Jewish High Priest on the night of his trial, he declared that he was the Son of God. Upon hearing these words Caiaphas tore his priestly garments. At that moment, through his unbelieving act, he lost his authority as God's accepted High Priest and his ministry at an earthly temple was rejected. God had now replaced him with another High Priest, someone who would never tear his priestly clothing, or those of his followers. Many would tear the clothes of Jesus, but he came to clothe the naked, not to tear their garments. On that day, Jesus was seen to be God's true High Priest by all the priesthood in Jerusalem. Through Christ's ministry, as the Father's accepted High Priest, His followers can also be clothed in the Garments of God and may function as priests of the Most High.

*John 19:23-24 'This garment was seamless, woven in one piece from top to bottom. "Let's not tear it." They said.'*

Whilst Christ's outer clothing was torn apart, there was another hidden garment that he was wearing underneath. Although unseen by human eyes, it was a perfect, seamless, linen garment of great value. It was the garment of a Priest. Even as Caiaphas tore his robe, the Son of God stood with his priestly garment intact. Jesus' ministry as God's true High Priest was about to be completed for all eternity, and he wore the garment to prove it. No one would tear this garment. God would not permit the perfect ministry of his son to be spoiled. Even the legionaries at Calvary instinctively acknowledged the value of this item of clothing and that it was too costly to be torn. Whilst all the soldiers were guilty of crucifying the Son of God, one of them, by divine providence, would receive a gift of great value. That fortunate soldier would be chosen to wear the garment of God. Instead of being condemned as a murderer, God's forgiveness meant that he would be blessed by receiving something of great value. That solitary soldier stands as a representative of everyone who comes to the cross of Christ. Whilst deserving punishment for their sins, they instead receive mercy and are clothed with salvation. Instead of being banished from God's presence forever, Christ's sacrifice enables the true believers to wear his priestly garment and be accepted by God.

# 4

## Priestly Garment

*'Make sacred garments for your brother Aaron and his sons so they may serve me as priests.'*

### *Exd. 28:4*

*C*onsiderable information is provided in scripture concerning the details of the garments of the priests. Two whole chapters are written in the book of Exodus alone giving details about every specific aspect of priests' clothing. Most of this information about the priests' garments can seem superfluous upon first glance and is often glossed over by many Christians when reading the Bible. The priests' clothes however, provide essential information to every believer who seeks to serve God. Jesus not only saves those who follow him, he also makes them priests in his Kingdom.[51] The clothes of the priests provide an essential metaphor for every Christian who desires to function in a way that pleases God. Only those who are dressed as a priest may enter God's Holy place.

---

51      1 Pet. 2:9

*Exd. 28:39-41 'Weave the tunic of fine linen and make the turban of fine linen…put these clothes on your brother Aaron and his sons, anoint and ordain them.'*

The garment of the priest was made of fine linen and everyone could immediately recognise a true priest of God by the clothes he wore. The anointing and ordination of a priest could only take place once they were dressed in fine linen. Priests had to wear the linen to cover the body and the turban for the head. It is amazing to remember that when Jesus rose from the dead, he left two items behind: the linen sheet covering his body and the linen cloth covering his head.[52] These are the garments Jesus expects his servants to wear as they serve him today. God always provides his children with the appropriate clothing necessary for their access to his presence. Even Samuel, a man ordained to serve God from birth, was continually supplied with the linen garment that he needed to serve at God's Tabernacle.[53] In the same way, at whatever stage or level of service a Christian is at, God supplies his children with the priestly clothes so they may minister before him. The garments are a designation of the heart and character of the individual who wears them. They are a sign to denote the true heart condition of anyone who claims to serve

---

52      John 20:6-7
53      1 Sam. 2:18-19

God. Just as a priest's garment was washed with water, so a believer's heart has been purified by God's grace.

*Exd. 29:21 'Take some blood from the altar and some of the anointing oil and sprinkle it on Aaron and his garments and on his sons and their garments. Then he and his sons and their garments will be consecrated.'*
Unless a believer is covered by the blood of the lamb, they cannot be righteous before God. In the Old Testament this was not a mere concept of belief, but a physical enactment. The blood was literally sprinkled on the garments of a priest. They had to be cleansed by the purity of the blood because 'without the shedding of blood there is no forgiveness.'[54]

**If the clothes are not correct, the anointing will not be applied.**

Unless this procedure was performed, the priest was rejected by God. Only if the blood was on the clothes of Aaron's sons could they be counted as righteous and consecrated to be set apart for priestly duty. Once the blood was sprinkled onto the garments, only then could the anointing oil also be applied. The anointing of the Holy Spirit will only come upon the garment of an individual when they have been declared righteous by the blood of Christ.

---

54        Heb.9:22

Today, many people crave a special anointing from God, but fail to realise that the anointing oil had to be placed on the garments of the priests.[55] The Holy Spirit will not clothe something just because man decides it is acceptable. If the clothes are not correct, the anointing will not be applied. The Psalms[56] clearly record that the anointing oil had to come down upon the robes of the priests' garments. Unfortunately, too many people desire anointing with power, but fail to wear the garments of God. To be anointed without developing a Godly character can end in disaster. The result of this is a faulty priesthood, corrupted by carnality, which will ultimately be rejected by God.

*Deut. 22:11 'Do not wear clothes of wool and linen woven together.'*
The garment of the priest must be pure linen, it cannot be combined with other materials. Ezekiel stressed that all God's priests must be clothed only in linen, as wool would make them perspire.[57] Sweat was a sign of God's original curse on mankind's sin[58] and must not be present in Christ's new order of priesthood. When someone serves God as a priest, every aspect of sin has to be removed. Even the aroma of sweat must be banished when serving in the Holy Temple. Every sign of man's former

---

55      Lev. 8:30
56      Psalm 133:2
57      Ezek. 44:17-19
58      Gen. 3:19

fallen state is not permitted in God's presence.

Too many people attempt to wear mixed garments when serving God today. They combine elements of true service to God, with aspects of their own ambition and selfish desires. They fail to realise that these Garments will never be accepted by God. God is looking for priests who are dressed in Christ's Garments and who have ceased from labouring through their own carnality to obtain success. They no longer sweat, as they are resting in the finished works of Christ. Their ministry flows out of the rest[59] that they have attained in being seated with Christ[60] and it does not come from their own lust for personal fulfilment and self-promotion. They don't confuse God's perfect will with their own carnal cravings. They don't mix wool with linen, but are content to wear the pure robe that Jesus has provided for them.

*Exd. 28:43 'Aaron and his sons must wear them whenever they...minister in the Holy Place, so that they will not incur guilt and die.'*

Most Christians recognise that they can only enter God's presence if the sacrifice on the altar is accepted as pure and clean. Whilst this is true, the offering could be accepted on the one hand, but the priest be rejected on

---

59      Matt. 11:28
60      Eph. 2:6

the other. The priest's acceptance was dependant on which garment they were wearing. Only the authentic garments of the priest were classified as holy by God. All Other types of clothing were not permitted in God's sanctuary. The Priest's garments represent the robes of Christ. All other carnal clothing is rejected when serving God. When the priests went outside God's temple precincts, they had to change their clothes.[61] Whilst outside the presence of God, the ordinary clothing of the world could be worn. The Holy Garments, however, could not be contaminated by the world but had to be left in God's presence.[62]

It is not good enough for a believer to say they will serve God when they refuse to be adorned in a way that pleases God. This does not mean there should be an emphasis on a physical dress code when attending church. The garment of God is a spiritual covering, not a religious uniform. It is a metaphor that points to a far more important principle that God has instructed his priests to observe. The priest's garment represents the true spiritual condition of every believer in the sight of God. Every form of sin must be judged by a Holy God and all aspects of the human carnal nature must die when entering the glory of God. Every aspect of fallen humanity represents dirty clothes[63] to God and no one dressed in this way

---

61      Lev.6:10-11
62      Lev. 16:23
63      Isa. 64:6

can ever meet his holy requirements. Standards accepted by the world are rejected when entering God's hallowed courts. Aaron's sons Nadab and Abihu wore the correct priestly garments but were still rejected due to the condition of their hearts.[64] God sees the heart.

*Zec. 3:4 '"Take off his filthy clothes." Then he said to Joshua, "See, I have taken away your sin, and I will put rich garments on you."'*

Even Joshua, Israel's high priest, had to have his filthy garments removed before he could wear the clean clothes that granted him access into God's temple. The priest's clothes cannot be worn over worldly carnality, which is filthy in God's sight. The aspects of human flesh may be hidden to men, but they are abhorrent to God. Jealousy, envy, hatred and selfish ambition are just a sample of what the apostle Paul calls the acts of the flesh.[65] Anyone exhibiting these characteristics in their life is dressed in flesh and unfit to wear the clothes of a priest. They may be hidden in the heart, just as filthy clothes are unseen underneath clean garments, but God sees them and his judgement is the same. No access will be permitted to one inappropriately dressed. Only by wearing the Holy garments of Christ can anyone come to God's altar and enter his temple. God will only hear

---

64      Numb. 10:1
65      Gal. 5:19-21

the prayers of his priests when they are wearing his robes.

*Isa. 61:3 'Bestow on them ...a garment of praise instead of the spirit of despair.'*

The old clothes were contaminated with despair and heaviness. The old clothes were reminders of death and destruction. The old clothes could not cause rejoicing as they gave no hope of renewal, but would wear out and be discarded. When someone belongs to Christ, however, they are clothed as a priest and the old mindset of depression, anxiety and hopelessness has been removed.

One of the primary duties of a priest was to give thanks and praise to God.[66] Praise is not just something that a Christian does, it is a garment they wear. Despair and hopelessness are not attitudes acceptable for God's priests, as they represent the old clothes that Christ has removed. God bestows the garment of praise that enables all his children to be filled with hope, due to the indwelling of his Holy Spirit. Death and destruction were removed when Christ clothed them with his salvation.

---

66      1 Chron. 16:4

*2 Chron. 6:41 'May your priests, O LORD God, be clothed with salvation.'*
God's priests don't just declare God's salvation, they are clothed in it. Too many people spend their lives trying to explain their salvation, when God expects us to wear it. In the Old Testament, you could tell that a priest belonged to God because of the clothes he wore. Everything about them declared God's salvation and, filled with joy, they gave thanks and sang God's praise.[67] When King David wore the linen garment, nothing could prevent him from dancing before the Lord and praising him with all his might.[68] When any individual understands the privilege of being able to wear the linen garment of God's priest, they too will manifest the joy of their salvation. Losing this spiritual covering was the greatest fear that David had.[69] God's garment cannot be worn without it producing an immediate effect upon the wearer. Their joy will be undeniable and their life will exhibit the characteristics of a true Priest of God.

---

67      Psalm 132:9
68      2 Sam. 16:14
69      Psalm 51:11

# 5

---

# King's Garment

*'In the year that king Uzziah died, I saw the Lord seated on a throne, high and exalted, and the train of his robe filled the temple.'*

### Isa 6:1

*H*aving just witnessed the death of Israel's earthly King, Isaiah saw the real king enthroned in Heaven and in the temple. He saw Jesus who was both a priest and a king.

When Isaiah entered the temple, you would have expected him to see a priest, as that was where they belonged. Instead, he had a vision of Jesus seated as a king on a throne, and the main thing that he noticed about him was the garment that he was wearing. On earth Jesus wore the linen garment of a priest, but in heaven he also wears the robe of the King. Jesus has always been the king, but many do not recognise him as such. One of the main reasons why people did not accept his kingship on earth, was because he was not dressed as a monarch when he walked the land of Israel. Man always looks at the outward, but God sees the inward reality.[70] Those who perceive things by the Spirit readily accept the Royalty of the Son of God. Like Isaiah, they have had a vision of the King and recognise him by the robes he wears. They know that he is clothed with 'splendour and majesty'[71] and that all his 'robes are fragrant with myrrh and aloes and cassia from palaces adorned with ivory.'[72] The robes that he wears declare that Jesus is the King of Kings.

### Roman Robe

*John 19:2-3 'They clothed him in a purple robe and went up to him again and again saying "Hail king of the Jews!" And they struck him in the face.'*

Rome controlled the known world in the time of Jesus and the Roman soldiers recognised no other king but Caesar. The political system of the Roman Empire ruled the world for hundreds of years and, during the first century A.D., Caesar was acknowledged as both an emperor and a god. Caesar alone was the supreme ruler over the Jews and Jesus, the despised leader from Nazareth, would never be accepted as a rival to Rome's monarch.

---

70      1 Sam. 16:7
71      Psalm 45:3
72      Psalm 45:8

Just as it was two thousand years ago, the kingship of Jesus is mocked and ridiculed by the people of this present age. Some will accept that he was a good religious leader or spiritual guru, but will not believe he is Lord and king. Today's leaders feel he has no business in the real politics of this world. His sermons and parables of God's kingdom may be seen as commendable ideals, but are totally impractical in the day to day kingdom of mankind. The only royal robe that is offered to Jesus by this world is the same one that the Romans gave him, a garment of mockery and spite. The only crown placed upon his head was a painful crown of thorns. After mocking him with robes of royalty, they stripped him naked and crucified him. They scorned his claims to real kingship and ensured he was stopped from interfering with their system of royal authority by removing him from their political system.

The present governments of the nations have not changed much from the systems of the Roman Empire. Politicians try to use Jesus as a tool to obtain more votes, but they will never lift him up as the king. It is often the president or the prime minister who today want to be dressed as Caesar and, they can believe, Jesus must play his part in enthroning them. They fail to recognise his royal robes and fail to acknowledge that it is only by accepting Jesus as King, that they can receive him at all. However, Jesus did not come to merely be a priest who would pray and intercede for the sin of mankind, he also came as the only person who was good enough, and fit to be, the ruler of the earth. God has clearly said 'I have installed MY king'[73] and he will never change his mind. Most people fail to recognise his royal robes and many others only give him a 'token' of homage at religious ceremonies. God, however, is looking for those who know that only Jesus wears the kingly robes of righteousness and that only he is fit to reign over the affairs of man.

### Jewish Robe

*Luke 23:11 'Then Herod and his soldiers ridiculed and mocked him, dressing him in in elegant robe.'*

It was not only the international political authorities that rejected the King-ship of Jesus. Small state governments would also despise his claims. Herod was the residing 'King of the Jews' and neither was he going to accept anyone taking his throne. Herod may have worn the crown and used the title, but he had no genuine claim to be Israel's king. Despite his lack of legitimate claim to the throne, he was going to make sure that he alone would wear the royal robes in Israel. Jesus would only be robed in clothes of imitation and mockery.

It must not be assumed that it was only the local politicians and Roman

---

73       Psalm 2:6

authorities that rejected Christ's kingship. The Jewish temple priests, as well as the Herodian monarch, also refused to acknowledge Jesus as king. The combined systems of human leadership and government, secular as well as religious, would not tolerate Jesus being their leader.

Herod and the Jewish leadership did not mind that Jesus did miracles, but they would never accept that he could be Israel's ruler. The same is true today. Of course, secular government has little time for Jesus being accepted as ruler, but many illegitimate 'kings,' like Herod, also reject Christ's absolute Lordship. In a world full of 'Christian' organisations and 'kingdoms,' many self-imposed 'kings' act as though they are in control of religious affairs instead of Jesus. Even many churches and denominations appoint their own 'supreme leaders' and dress them up as kings whilst paying mock homage to the true ruler of the church. Whilst claiming to be shepherds of God's flock, many pastors actually act more like kings and expect to be treated like royalty by 'ordinary' members of the church. These deluded dictators rarely seek genuine guidance from God in fulfilling their ministries, but instead assume that their appointment gives them free reign to behave as local despots. If these self-appointed monarchs had an authentic encounter with God's presence, they would strip off their self-made royal robes, like King Saul, and fall on their face in worship to the true king.[74]

*Acts 12:21-23 'Herod, wearing his royal robes, sat on his throne...*
*immediately, because Herod did not give praise to God, an angel of the*
*Lord struck him down.'*

Once he had mocked and rejected God's true king, Herod clung to his

earthly throne and insisted on wearing his royal robes as an outward sign

of his position and prestige. He mistakenly thought that his human robes

would give his kingship permanence and security. He failed to recognise

that true royal position in life only

exists when Jesus is made king. Despite

the passing of two thousand years since

Herod's fatal miscalculation, many

people follow his failed example instead

of the one set by Jesus. They love to

> *He mistakenly thought that his human robes would give his kingship permanence and security.*

wear the royal robes of this life rather than bowing the knee to Christ's

kingship. There can only be one king reigning in the heart of each person.

It is either Christ or themselves. It is also true that only one king can rule

over each church, and it is not the Pastor. Senior leaders of every Christian

organisation must take to heart the lesson of Herod. While it is essential

---

74      1 Sam. 19:24

to encourage leaders, praise and glory belongs to God alone. No pastor should ever wear the royal robes of glory that belong only to God. Even the good King Jehoshaphat almost lost his life when he went into battle wearing unnecessary royal robes.[75] Self-aggrandisement makes you an easy target for the enemy to aim at. Unfortunately, in the present age of image and status, leaders can easily fall into the trap of selfish promotion, entitlement and self-honour. The results of such adornment lead to increased pride and narcissism, which inevitably result in judgement and destruction. A haughty spirit always goes before a fall.[76]

*2 Sam. 6:20 'How the king of Israel has distinguished himself today, disrobing…as any vulgar fellow would.'*

When King David worshipped God, he was happy to discard his earthly royal robes so that he could be unhindered to dance in God's presence. True leaders with genuine hearts after God follow his example. It is true that carnal Christians will always criticise leadership that does not fit into their prescribed level of dignity, but authentic ministers focus on the inner reality and not the outward appearance. David's own wife wanted him to be limited by her family's prescribed traditions. She considered

75       2 Chron. 18:29-32
76       Prov. 16:18

his choice of clothing and act of service as vulgar and unacceptable. She expected him to wear the traditional royal garment that accommodated her own level of prestige, but the king would have none of it. David's praise was focused on giving God the glory and not on promoting his own outward image and reputation. David would remove earthly royal robes in order to wear the garment of God. That is why God loved him so much.

God always sees the heart. In the spiritual realm, out-ward adornment is useless. When King Saul removed his royal robes and disguised himself when seeking counsel from the witch of Endor, the spirit within her knew immediately that he was the king regardless of how he was dressed.[77] As looked at earlier, she also identified Samuel by the garment he was wearing. Spirits recognise the reality of a person's true garment, not their outward pretence. Demons were cast out when Paul's clothing was placed on tormented people, because the evil spirits knew his genuine apostolic power and authority.[78] When 'false exorcists' tried to cast out demons, the spirits immediately recognised that they had no real authority. The Sons of Sceva had their clothes stripped from them and were left naked when they attempted to use royal authority that they did not possess.[79]

---

77      1 Sam. 28:8-14
78      Acts 19:12
79      Acts 19:13-16

Demonic Spirits always know the difference between those who wear an authentic royal robe and those who have a fake one. Everyone will discover, like King Saul, that when entering God's presence all false royal robes will have to be removed.

## *The Royal Robe in this life*

*Esther 6:7-9 'For the man the king delights to honour, have them bring a royal robe the king has worn…let them robe the man the king delights to honour.'*

True leaders will not exalt themselves by adorning their bodies with royal robes, but many are still recognised in this world for their sincere service and authentic righteousness. True leaders will sometimes receive royal garments of honour, even in this earthly life, and be bestowed with adulations of men, despite them not seeking it for themselves. God delights to honour his humble servants.

In the book of Esther, Mordecai was a faithful servant to his master and always worked for the good of others. He protected the king, watched over his family and continually worked for the benefit of God's people. When a day came where he had to wear a royal robe, it did not puff him up with pride. On the contrary, as soon as he had been clothed with the king's garment, he received it with gratitude, but then immediately

resumed his mundane duties of service at the king's gate.[80] Power did

not go to his head. Even when he was exalted, he retained the attitude of

a servant. When men bestow prestigious titles upon servants of God, it

should never affect their character or attitude. Even when called bishop,

apostle or prophet, the heart must remain pure. Giving thanks to God

for allowing them to be honoured, they should continue to serve in

thankfulness and humility. It is only by grace beyond comprehension that

anyone may wear a royal robe, let alone one worn by the king of kings.

If a Christian is exalted in this life, they should give thanks and use the

opportunity to represent their king and speak on behalf of his people.

*Esther 5:1 'Esther put on her royal robes…and stood in front of the king.'*
Wearing a royal robe in this life is sometimes essential to fulfilling God's

plan for his people. God had ordained it that Esther would become Queen

and would wear the clothes of royalty. In the beginning of her royal life,

Esther did not seem to appreciate why she had been elevated to such a

prominent position. She would later realise that God had planned it all

along, so that she would be in the right place at the right time to help

others. For a season, she seemed to be content living her privileged life

---

80        Esth. 6:12

in the king's palace, but a day arrived when her royal garments would be necessary to fulfil God's plan for her life and her nation.

One critical day, she was told that she had 'come to royal position for such a time as this.'[81] At that time she had a choice to make. Would she continue to live her life of elevated privilege in the same way as she always had, or would she dress in her royal robes and ask the king to save her people? When the king saw his bride dressed in her royal robes, he immediately stated he would answer her request. Esther had not even spoken, but the king saw the one he loved wearing the garments that he had provided. Upon seeing his royal bride in her beautiful robes, he gave her grace and favour in her time of need.[82]

When God's people approach their king in times of crisis, they must enter his presence wearing the correct garments. No Christian must ever think that honoured positions in this life are given for their own selfish indulgence. They must use every opportunity afforded to them to serve God clothed in the garment he has provided. When the Royal garment is worn, Heaven's king will never fail to answer the need.

---

81      Esth. 4:14
82      Heb. 4:16

*Rev. 19:13 'He is dressed in a robe dipped in Blood, and his name is the Word of God...On his robe and on his thigh he has this name written: KING OF KINGS AND LORD OF LORDS.'*

Even though no one recognised the royalty of Jesus at his first coming, everyone will see it at his second advent. There will be no mistaking who he is. His Robes will declare his majesty. In the Old Testament, no one was allowed into Temple of God's presence unless their garments were sprinkled with blood.[83] Jesus' robes have been dipped in blood because he is returning from the presence of his father. He is not returning as a lamb that was slain, but as a lion to rule as king.[84] God the Father has crowned him, enthroned him and robed him in royal garments. The declaration of his kingship is embroidered upon his robes, so that there will be no mistaking who he is. Everyone will bow down to the true King.

---

83      Lev. 8:30
84      Rev. 5:5

*Isa. 63:1-3 'Who is this,..with his garments stained crimson? Who is this, robed in splendour?...Why are your garments red?..."I have trodden the winepress alone;.. I trampled them in my anger and trod them down in my wrath; their blood spattered my garments and I stained all my clothing.""*

The prophets predicted a day when the Messiah would return. At his second coming, his garments would be very different from those he wore when he first walked the earth. On that Day, Jesus will be wearing the 'garments of vengeance.'[85] Two thousand years ago, he completed the ministry of priest by offering his own perfect life as a sacrifice to atone for sins. When he returns, Jesus comes to reign as King and to punish all acts of disobedience and rejection of his grace. Some acknowledged Jesus as king at his first coming when they 'spread their cloaks on the road.'[86] They understood all other individual garments must be put aside in recognition of the kingship of Christ. His true disciples accepted him as king and saviour. Those who reject Jesus as king cannot receive him as their saviour. Everyone, however, will have to face him as Judge.

When Jesus returns his garments will be those of justice and punishment. The evil that he conquered at the cross will finally be removed from the

---

85      Isa. 59:17
86      Luke 19:36

earth. All who rejected his grace will receive his righteous justice, and his judgement will be distributed to all people and nations that spurned his salvation. If Christ's garments of grace have been rejected, then all that remains is the expectation of wrath and punishment.[87] His royal clothes at his second advent will be very different from those worn at his first coming.

While in the world, Jesus was clothed in the humility of humanity and his servants are likewise dressed today. Jesus said that during his earthly ministry even John the Baptist, the greatest of men born of woman, did not wear luxurious clothes from a royal palace.[88] John lived in the desert and wore a different robe altogether. He wore the garment of a prophet.

87      Heb. 10:26-27
88      Matt. 11:8

# 6

## Prophet's Garment

*'"He was a man with a garment of hair and with a leather belt around his waist." The king said, "That was Elijah."'*

***2 Kings 1:8***

$A$ prophet was recognised by the garment he wore. It was a symbol of his office. As soon as the evil king of Israel heard what kind of clothes the messenger was wearing, he realised it was God's prophet and he knew that he would be rebuked for his wicked ways. The Priestly garment of linen kept the wearer cool and the royal robe was a symbol of honour. The Prophet's garment, however, was altogether different. It was neither soft nor refined, but coarse and hairy. It was purposefully prickly and uncomfortable in keeping with the nature of a prophet's ministry. Those called to wear the mantle of a prophet, will soon realise that their words make people feel uncomfortable. When speaking on behalf of God, a true prophet will always cause discomfort to carnal flesh. There is no point in complaining about the painful aspects of a prophet's ministry, they have purposely been called to rebuke kings and nations on behalf of God.

Many Christians enjoy wearing the clothes of the priest and hope to be adorned in the robes of a king. Far fewer believers put on the garment of the prophet, because they don't want to upset anybody. They are happy to pray for people and rule over people, but less inclined to rebuke sin in the lives of others. God does, however, offer his people the garment of a prophet. In some capacity, all Christians are expected to tell other people the truth about God. Prophets often offend and challenge carnal people and it is only when God's truth is spoken, that the irritating nature of their garment fully manifests itself.

*Matt. 11:8-9 'What did you go out to see? A man dressed in fine clothes? No, those who wear fine clothes are in kings' palaces. Then what did you go out to see? A prophet? Yes, I tell you, and more than a prophet.'*

People who genuinely want to hear the truth, seek out a prophet of God. Those looking for reality don't mind uncomfortable journeys into the desert, as their overriding purpose is to hear the word of the Lord. They don't care how uncouth and rugged the prophet is, their sole desire is to hear and obey God. When the people travelled to hear John the Baptist, there was no beautiful, air-conditioned building for them to rest in from the stifling humidity of the Jordan valley. They journeyed to the lowest point on earth, because they needed to hear the prophet who was preparing God's people to meet their Messiah.

God clothes his prophets in abrasive garments today. They are seldom found in royal palaces or lavish temples, as they do not pander to the luxury-seeking spirit of the age. True prophets are only concerned with making sure that people hear the truth and are obedient to God's commands. The prophet's words cut like a knife into the hearts of their hearers. Those with priestly titles would be called 'snakes and vipers' and those sitting on thrones would be severely rebuked for their sinful lifestyle.[89] Those who believed, however, recognised that it was the voice of God and they were not put off by the uncultured nature and direct speech of the prophet.

*Mark 1:4 'John wore clothing made of camel's hair, with a leather belt around his waist, and he ate locusts and wild honey.'*

Dressed in the same garments as Elijah, John the Baptist was the greatest

---

89        Matt. 3:7

prophet born of women.[90]

Priests and kings hated him and the garment that he wore. His clothing was a direct rebuke to their luxurious and selfish lifestyle. What is amazing to note, is that John the Baptist belonged to the priestly tribe of Levi. His Father, Zechariah, was a righteous man who had worn the priestly linen garments while serving in God's temple.[91] John had every legal right to wear the same clothes and take the official titles that had been handed down by his family. The prophet, however, rejected the religious temple system that had become corrupt and

> *False leaders hate the prophet's message and the garment he wears*

defiled. The priests no longer functioned in a righteous way and the whole religious system had become an economic and political system, oppressing the poor to keep an entitled elite in positions of power. Filled with the Holy Spirit from birth, John was called to wear the garment of hair and speak against the fallen Levitical priest-hood. He would prepare the way for God's true priest who would imminently arrive on the scene. John was no hypocrite; his words matched his clothes and his lifestyle. His garments were simple and his diet was basic. He ate Locusts and

90      Matt. 11:11
91      Luke 1:5

wild honey. Honey is always a picture of God's coming promise. The Promised Land was flowing with honey and the manna in the desert tasted like honey.[92] God used honey to reveal to his children that they could taste now, what was yet to come. Despite John's rough exterior, he held out a great hope to God's people. He reminded them the Messiah was near and that they needed to be ready to enter his kingdom.

At the same time as promising the honey, he also ate locusts! One is sweet, but the other is rather unpalatable to refined tastes. This is interesting, because in the Bible locusts can be a picture of demons and unclean spirits[93] which were said to inhabit the desert.[94] John the Baptist lived in the desert and promised a sweet hope, while at the same time destroying demons. He did not hide from the forces of evil but confronted them in their own territory. John preached that God's promise was sure, but evil still had to be put away. The kingdom of grace was near, but everyone still needed to repent.[95] There would be no forgiveness without obedience.

Satan may tolerate the fine robes of kings and priests, but he cannot ignore the prophet's garment. He always tries to kill the prophet, and he often succeeds. Elijah escaped by running away, but John the Baptist lost his head because he spoke the truth and rebuked a king. False leaders hate

---

92      Exd. 16:31
93      Rev. 9:3
94      Matt. 12:43
95      Mark 1:14

the prophet's message and the garment he wears. They especially despise

the belt of the prophet and all that it symbolises.

### The Prophet's Belt

*Acts 21:10-11 'A prophet named Agabus came down from Judea. Coming*

*over to us, he took Paul's belt, tied his own hands and feet with it and*

*said..."The Jews of Jerusalem will bind the owner of this belt."'*

The leather belt of the prophet is hated by Satan. Just like John the Baptist

and Elijah, Paul also had prophetic gifting. Wearing the leather belt meant

that people would also seek his death. This came as no surprise to Paul,

as he had been told by God at his initial conversion that he would have to

suffer much for being his spokesman.[96]  When it is understood what the

belt represents, it is easy to see why Satan despises this piece of clothing

so much and why he tries to remove it from God's people.

*Eph. 6:14 'Stand firm then, with the belt of truth buckled around your*

*waist.'*

The belt represents truth. Nothing was more prominent in a prophet's

ministry than that he proclaimed the truth. Satan is a liar and the father

---

96       Acts 9:16

of lies[97] and, consequently, he cannot tolerate truth. It demolishes everything he stands for and he must, at all costs, remove the belt of truth from the prophet. If he can make the prophet compromise with truth, then his message can be discredited and Satan's deception can be accepted. A true prophet, however, will never water down the truth. Whatever the cost to his own life he must preach the truth, for only the truth can set people free.[98]

*1 Kings 18:46 'The power of the LORD came upon Elijah and, tucking his cloak into his belt, he ran.'*

Another reason that Satan tries to remove the belt is due to its essential connection to the other garments. The function of the prophet's belt is to hold all the other garments together. Truth binds everything together. Without the belt, all the clothes of the prophet begin to unravel and fall off. As soon as anyone lets go of truth, all other beliefs become merely subjective or irrelevant. Instead of wearing the belt of absolute truth, some people become ungirded and fall into the deception of moral relativism. A true prophet will never remove his belt. Once someone has become deceived believing there is no absolute truth, they soon unravel

---

97      John 8:44
98      John 8:32

and become totally unclothed, ending up in the same naked state as Adam and Eve after their deception.

*2 Kings 4:29 'Elisha said to Gehazi, "Tuck your cloak in your belt…and run."'*

All young prophets must listen to the wisdom of the older generation. Anyone called to a prophetic ministry must never forget to wear the belt of truth. Without the belt, the prophet's ministry is useless. No one can run with a message from God without fastening the belt tightly around them. The other garments will quickly fall down and ministry will be tripped up without it. All ministry becomes useless if not held together by truth. No one can let go of truth and continue to serve God. The prophet knows that God's words are absolute truth and he has to preach them in the full and confident conviction that, despite man's opposition, God will always vindicate his word.

### *False Prophets*

*Zech. 13:4 'On that day every prophet will be ashamed of their prophetic vision. They will not put on a prophet's garment of hair in order to deceive.'*

The Bible warns against false prophets as much as it expects people to listen to genuine ones. The apostle Peter warned the church that it would be infiltrated with false prophets and teachers.[99] They will be very cunning in their deception and their spiritual antics will appear to clothe them in the same fashion that a true prophet would be dressed. Their teaching may seem innocent in the first instance, but slowly, it will reveal itself to be a creeping heresy that will ensnare God's people. It is essential that the church is able to discern the difference between true and false prophets and the Bible gives critical advice in spotting the difference. They are identified in the garments that they wear.

*Matt. 7:15 'Watch out for false prophets. They come to you in sheep's clothing, but inwardly they are ferocious wolves.'*

Jesus said that you can spot a false prophet by the clothes that they wear. A true prophet is clothed in a camel's garment, but a false prophet wears wool. True prophets irritate and challenge carnality, but the woollen false garment is soft and comfortable to the flesh. False prophets do not offend the flesh, they flatter it. They preach a grace without truth. They prophesy sensual satisfaction to appease the sinful human condition and, in doing so, can accumulate many followers. Fallen humanity is always looking for leaders that will give them what they want, instead of what God requires.

---

99        2 Pet. 2:1

People have always given platforms to false prophets who will feed them what they crave. Micah predicted that, 'If a liar and deceiver comes and says, "I will prophesy for you plenty of wine and beer," that would be just the prophet for this people!'[100] These lying prophets are dressed in wool, so that outwardly they look like sheep and, a true member of Christ's flock, but that is not their real condition. God's anointed leaders were not allowed to wear wool.[101] These deceivers are not woolly sheep, but wolves.

*Acts 20:29 'Savage wolves will come in among you and will not spare the flock.'*

Wolves are very different from sheep. They do not want to feed the sheep, but want to eat them. Paul understood this and warned the Ephesian elders about false prophets entering the church. If these false prophets arose in the Godly church at Ephesus with all of its apostolic input and Biblical teaching, they will certainly come into the worldly fellowships of today. Paul said these manipulators would even arise from within the flock. Wolves always exhibit specific characteristics that are easy to spot. They prey on the weak and vulnerable and snarl when they do not get their own

100    Micah 2:11
101    Ezek. 44:17

way. True pastors can spot the wolves, and they use their powers to keep them from having any influence over God's flock. Wolves can usually be seen to behave differently when the shepherd is absent and will seek to undermine pastoral authority in order to feed on the sheep themselves. They change their behaviour depending on who is watching. When the Pastor is absent, the true nature of the wolves can be discerned. People must learn to spot the nature of the garment that a prophet is wearing. Those clothed with wool are hiding the carnivore's coat underneath and are seeking things for themselves. Those wearing the true prophet's garment are always pointing people towards Jesus and not themselves.

### *Passing the Prophet's Mantle*

*2 Kings 2:12-14 '[Elisha] took hold of his own clothes and tore them into two pieces. He also took up the mantle of Elijah that had fallen from him...He took the mantle of Elijah that had fallen from him and struck the water.' (NKJ)*

Before a prophetic mantle can be used, every garment of the old nature has to be torn off and discarded. A prophetic ministry cannot be mixed between spirit and flesh. When Elisha first touched Elijah's cloak (when he was called many years before), he had to leave his home, his family and his profession. When Elijah threw his cloak over Elisha as a young man,[102] it began his prophetic training, but it would take years to complete. After decades of faithful service, the day arrived when Elisha would also have to lose all his own clothing, because there is no power in anything of the old nature. The supernatural anointing required for his future prophetic ministry would only be found in wearing the attested prophet's mantle. The genuine ministry of the prophet can only be realised when the old clothes are destroyed and the new mantle is worn. Elisha knew the value of his master's mantle. This was the same cloak that Elijah had worn on the mountain of God.[103] It was the very robe that had covered Elijah's face when he stood in the presence of the glory. Elisha knew it's true value and understood that it would protect and cover him, just as it had his master.

*2 Kings 2:13 'He picked up the cloak that had fallen from Elijah.'*
Every ministry from God must follow a divine pattern and procedure of succession. The garment of every true servant of God must be passed onto the next generation. The prophetic mantle that was placed upon Elisha at his initial call would only fall upon him in succession if he

---

102      1 Kings 19:19
103      1 Kings 19:13

remained faithful in his walk and service to his master. Elisha called Elijah 'my father'[104] not 'my boss.' He was in a genuine relationship with his senior leader, not merely doing a job as a means to future promotion. Genuine anointed ministry is only passed on to faithful sons. This is true in the prophetic ministry as well as every other type of service. When Aaron was about to die, the garment of the high priest was taken from him and placed on his son, who then faithfully succeeded him in the tabernacle.[105] When David was near death, the king's anointing and possessions were given to his son Solomon.[106] The Bible always reveals that good fathers provide the best robes for their sons. Anointed garments were only given to those who served in humility and faithfulness. They were never automatically given to anyone who claimed them, nor were they passed on to those who snatched or promoted themselves into them. True servants of God always endeavour to wear the garment of service.

---

104     2 Kings 2:12
105     Numb. 20:28
106     1 Kings 1:33-37

# 7

## Servant's Garment

*'Jesus got up from the meal, took off his outer clothing, and wrapped a towel around his waist.'*

### John 13:4

*C*hristians very much desire to wear the garments of prophets, priests and king's. They may imagine that wearing such clothing will increase their prestige in the eyes of the world. In their eagerness to enter into God's ministry, however, they often overlook the fact that, in order to succeed, these roles require the attitude of a servant. Jesus was the greatest prophet, priest and king to ever walk the earth, but he was simultaneously the perfect servant. He never allowed his disciples to believe that wearing ministry garments was a short cut to promoting their own honour and prestige. The Bible emphasised that he 'made himself nothing, taking the very nature of a servant'[107] and declared that Jesus was 'among you

---

107      Phil. 2:7

as one who serves.'[108] To cement the reality of ministry in the minds of his followers, Jesus disrobed and dressed himself as a slave. He took off his outer robes and clothed himself with a towel, a garment of a servant.

*2 Kings 5:26 'Is this the time to take money, or accept clothing.'*

As shown earlier, when Elisha received Elijah's robe[109] he accepted the calling to be a servant. He poured water on his master's hands for many years before inheriting his prophetic mantle, and this would only be confirmed if he remained faithful to Elijah until the end of his ministry. There are no shortcuts in genuine ministry and all appointments from God are a call to service. Hard work, done in sincerity, is what God is looking for in his ministers and 'deeds done in humility'[110] are greatly valued in his sight. When a wealthy government leader offered Elisha the garments of success and prestige, he refused to accept them. He knew which ministry he was called to and would not change his robes of service, no matter how great the temptation.

Unfortunately, whilst Elisha set a good example, his assistant failed to grasp how the garment of service was to be worn. In the second book of Kings, the story of Gehazi is told. Many desire the titles associated

---

108     Luke 22:27
109     1 Kings 19:19
110     James 3:13

with ministry, but fail to follow the examples of God's humble servants. Gehazi should have been the next great prophet of Israel. He should have inherited Elisha's prophetic mantle and was next in line to step into this prestigious role. He had witnessed many miracles performed by his master and had first-hand knowledge of Elisha's power, wisdom and humility. He knew that, despite his great reputation, Elisha was a humble servant who simply obeyed his God. Regrettably, Gehazi failed to emulate his pastor and deceitfully schemed to obtain the clothing that looked good in his own eyes.

*2 Kings 5:21-22 'Gehazi hurried after Naaman…please give…a talent of silver and two sets of clothes.'*

This is all Gehazi asked from Namaan after Elisha had cured him of leprosy. Surely it was not too much to ask? Was not 'a worker due his wages?'[111] Accepting a gift was not the sin, but his deceitful manipulation and disobedience to his leader's instructions was unacceptable. Gehazi knew that his master had forbidden the taking of this gentile clothing. He did not just take one robe, but asked for 'two sets of clothing,' something the Lord himself has forbidden.[112] God's prophets could not be seen to

---

111     1 Tim. 5:18
112     Mark 6:9

be wearing a Babylonian or Assyrian robe. Gehazi knew this, but chose his own path nevertheless. When his master was not looking, Gehazi embarked upon his own scheme of obtaining a robe for himself rather, than faithfully waiting for the mantle to be passed from above. He also pretended that the garments were for the benefit of someone else, which was not true. In Elisha's presence he would act like his servant, but when his back was turned, he would endeavour to ensure that he would get the clothes that he wanted. Like the young priest in the book of Judges, he would prostitute his ministry for shekels and a shirt.[113]

Many young ministers follow Gehazi's bad example today. They are bored with faithfully serving a pastor in a local church and impatiently try to wear the garment of a higher ministry before being fully clothed as a servant. They want a shortcut to honour and prestige, so they pretend to serve in public whilst secretly scheming to promote themselves behind the scenes. It is easy to set up a web site and name a ministry after oneself declaring their special anointing to the world, but it is much harder to serve in simplicity and sincerity trusting that God will exalt those he chooses.

Gehazi could not wait. He needed immediate gratification of his lustful desires. He wanted to look good in the eyes of the world and he believed

---

113      Judges 17:10

that Namaan's robes would clothe him in the appearance of success. He

*Gehazi embarked upon his own scheme of obtaining a robe for himself, rather than faithfully waiting for the mantle to be passed.*

lied to Namaan, and possibly himself, that the clothes would benefit other people; but his deceit would destroy him. Like Judas Iscariot after him, he pretended to be a servant while covertly arranging for his own selfish benefit. Such hypocritical service will always end in destruction. Claiming it will benefit others does not fool God or disguise the real motives of the heart. Judas hid his intentions from his master, just as Gehazi hid the forbidden clothing in his tent, but sin is always found out. Gehazi could keep his new clothing, but it would be of no benefit to him, as God would curse him with leprosy. His new garments would now have to be torn whenever he wore them, as that was the penalty of leprosy.[114]

Gehazi's problem was rooted in his disobedience to his master, as he thought he knew better. Instead of following Elisha's example and being clothed as a servant, he thought he was above his Pastor and deserved a higher level of attire. Service was just a means to an end for Gehazi, it

---

114      Lev. 13:45

was not his true attitude of heart. God was looking for a humble servant, but Gehazi wanted to dress to impress.


*2 Kings 7:8 'The men who had leprosy...carried away silver, gold and clothes and went off and hid them.'*

A Jewish tradition states that during the siege of Samaria, one of the lepers outside the city gate was Gehazi. If this is true, then it appears that his old selfish habits still clung to him. The first thing that these lepers did when faced with a golden opportunity, was to hide garments for themselves. This form of self-seeking was what got Gehazi into his unclean predicament in the first place. It was through hiding garments for himself that he became isolated and leprous. In the Bible, leprosy is a metaphor for man's old sinful nature. It represents the carnal soul that is self-seeking from birth. The reason Gehazi became unclean, was because he chose to seek and promote his own ministry instead of focusing on being a servant. Once an individual develops the habit and routine of self-promotion, they become increasingly less servant-hearted. Service to God is a garment that is worn, and so are the clothes of self-importance. No one can wear both cloaks at the same time. True servants are focussed on serving their leaders and the well-being of others, not seizing every opportunity to make themselves look better. Christian ministry is a genuine and authentic life of service, not a performance.

Even in the midst of trying to obtain the most expensive clothes for themselves, these lepers finally came to their senses. It is not clear how many garments they had hidden for themselves before they confessed to each other, 'We're not doing right.'[115] There is always hope that in the midst of the false riches this world offers, people can still perceive that life is not about what you can get, but what you can give. Jesus said that the clothes obtained in this life are here today and gone tomorrow.[116] This is obvious for everyone to see. A wasted life and much pain can be avoided when people follow Jesus' example and heed his words concerning what he accepts as true ministry. It comes from the simplicity of wearing the garment of a servant and not from trying to obtain another tunic as well.

## Luke 9:3 'Take nothing for the journey...no extra tunic.'

When Jesus sent out his twelve disciples, he gave them very clear instructions. They were not permitted to take an extra garment. If Jesus was only giving practical travel advice, then this tip for short-term missions did not make much sense. As always, Jesus was hinting towards a deeper meaning in his instructions. His disciples were being sent out

---

115      2 Kings 7:9
116      Matt. 6:28-33

on official ministry, so they would now be able to legitimately use the title of Apostle. Jesus knew that official titles could puff up the sinful nature into thinking it is more important than it is. To guard against pride manifesting in their hearts, he reminded them about the garment they wore. They were to function as his ambassadors, but they must not use this appointment to obtain another tunic. He was protecting them from falling into the same error of Gehazi; he wanted them to wear the garment of a servant and not seek to swap it for a more prestigious one.

*Num. 15:37-38 'Make tassels on the corners of your garments…You will have these tassels to look at and so you will remember all the commands of the LORD, that you may obey them and not prostitute yourselves by going after the lusts of your own heart and eyes.'*

The garments of God's people were always to serve as a reminder of their purpose on earth. God's children are here to serve God and not themselves. Every time they looked at their clothes they recalled the nature of their obligation to God. The tassels were a mnemonic which enabled the wearer to concentrate on living their life as a servant to the Lord. They cautioned against pride entering the heart and acted as a warning from seeking the lust of the eyes.

In the Gospels, when the woman required healing from blood loss,[117] she reasoned that all she needed to do to obtain her healing was to touch the edges of Jesus' cloak. How did she come to the conclusion that touching the hem of his garment would bring healing? Jesus had never preached about the edge of his clothes having healing properties. Perhaps this woman saw the tassels on the corner of his garments and recognised what they represented. She knew that here was a man who truly remembered God's commands and actually obeyed them. She believed that Jesus did not prostitute himself by seeking dishonest gain or follow the lust of his own satisfaction. She saw that Jesus was God's promised servant and that he wore the garments of service and, in her faith, she pushed through the crowd to touch his cloak.

When the garment of service and obedience is worn, true power is present. The tassels of the garment are a continual reminder that Christian ministry is to be carried out with a servant heart and never with motives for seeking selfish gain. Even in the midst of ministerial success, the tassels must remain on the garment of every Christian as a guard against pride.

---

117        Matt. 9:20-22, Luke 8:43-48

*Luke 12:35-36 'Be dressed ready for service...like men waiting for their master.'*

Jesus expects his people to be dressed in the garment of service. All Christians have duties to perform for God and other people. Sometimes, many Christians give excuses for not serving, but they usually fall short of God's expectations. Being clothed by God obligates the believer to help clothe others. As the great prophet declared, 'The man with two tunics should share with him who has none.'[118] One of the simplest ways of looking at service is to view it through the metaphor of the garment. Just as Christ has always clothed his followers, so his people should seek to provide garments for others. He gives us the perfect model to follow through his description of the wife of noble character, who is a picture of his faithful church.

*Prov.31:10-25 'A wife of noble character...She selects wool and flax and works...she opens her arms to the poor...all of them are clothed in scarlet...she is clothed in fine linen and purple...she makes linen garments...she is clothed with strength and dignity.'*

A true church fulfils the duties of the noble wife found in the book of proverbs. First of all, she is clothed in linen and purple that speaks of

---

118      Luke 3:11

the royal and priestly roles of the church. Secondly, she wears a robe of strength and dignity revealing that she is empowered to fulfil her duties. And thirdly, her primary ministries are outlined.

The primary ministry of the church is in reaching out to others to ensure that they have access to the same clothing enjoyed by God's children. It is the wife who selects the appropriate materials and she differentiates between wool and linen.[119] Wool could be used to make tents and other coverings, but she knows the Biblical restrictions on woollen garments. Having identified the correct materials, she makes linen garments. The church must not asssume that it can clothe people in any garment that seems appropriate. It cannot pick and choose its preferred paths of service; its activities must be in accordance with God's words of direction. Ministries must not be chosen just because they look good. As has been discussed in previous chapters, God wants his people dressed in linen, not wool.

Next, we find that the people she is reaching out to are the poor. Like Dorcas in the book of Acts, the noble church also makes 'robes and other clothing'[120] for the poor. God's people have a duty of care to help the poor. The church cannot show any prejudice to those whom God chooses

---

119      Linen is made from flax.
120      Acts 9:39

to be his children. The Apostle James rebuked the church for showing favouritism to those 'wearing fine clothes' while neglecting those in 'shabby clothes.'[121] All are of equal value in God's sight and Jesus specifically came to 'proclaim good news to the poor'.[122] His church must do likewise. It will be a terrifying experience for any unfaithful servant to hear Jesus' fearful words on the day of judgement, 'I needed clothes and you did not clothe me.'[123]

Finally, Proverbs says that that clothing is scarlet, the colour of blood. While the practical elements of social action and service must be present in a true church, they must never be at the expense of revealing the true message of the gospel. The garments of service were described as blood red. Everyone must understand the primary reason why the church provides clothing to others. It is because of the precious blood of Jesus. He shed his blood so that everyone could be included in the family of God. Every garment and every act of service must declare this fact. Without the grace that came from forgiveness, through his blood, no one could be clothed.

---

121     James 2:2-4
122     Luke 4:18
123     Matt 25:43

# 8

---

# Pastor's Garment

*'Jesus said, "Feed my sheep. I tell you the truth, when you were*
*younger you dressed yourself and went where you wanted; but when*
*you are old you will stretch out your hands, and someone else will dress*
*you.'*

### *John 21:17-18*

$A$ll God's children are expected to wear his garments. As has been
seen, all who belong to God are Kings and Priests[124] in his kingdom,
and they are provided with royal and priestly robes. Some of God's
people, however, are also called into specific roles of leadership in his
church. Jesus instructed his leaders to feed and look after his flock, and
those who watch over his sheep are called shepherd or Pastor.[125] It is
important to note that when Peter was commanded to fulfil his pastoral
role, Jesus instructed him in how he was to get dressed. There is a clear
link between the garment of the pastor and the nature of their ministry.

---

124      Rev. 1:6
125      Shepherd and Pastor are the same Greek word, poimen

By examining the attire of the leading Pastors in the New Testament, a greater understanding of this essential ministry can be revealed.

## *Peter*

Jesus instructed Peter that if he wanted to be a pastor of his flock, he could not expect to dress himself. This can appear to be a strange metaphor to use unless the importance of the pastor's garment is understood. Peter was indeed called to lead God's flock, but there was a serious flaw in his character that restricted his ability to fulfil his pastoral role. It is an issue that is found all too often in modern church leadership. The

*Peter realised he could not serve God and dress himself at the same time.*

problem is that Pastors often want to dress themselves according to their own opinions. They may want to be in charge of everything, directing everyone and choosing their own plans and vision. They can fall into the error of thinking that they are the head of the church and that they must determine where their ministry goes and what it will achieve. Peter had the same problem. He was strong-willed and ambitious. This sometimes led him to think that he could tell Jesus what kind of ministry to do.[126]

---

126      Matt. 16:22

*John 21:18 'Someone else will dress you and lead you where you do not want to go.'*

Wanting to express his personal opinions and plan the direction of his own ministry, continued to plague the life of Peter. When told by Jesus that his own strength would fail, he contradicted his master and asserted his own opinion.[127] When instructed to plant a Gentile church in Caesarea, he told God three times that, in his view, it was wrong.[128] The simple truth was that Peter did not want to go there, so he assumed that God did not want it either. It took a long time before Peter realised he could not serve God and dress himself at the same time. True ministry has to be totally directed by God. What it is, where it will be located and how it is to be carried out are all decided by God, not man.

Pastors are servants of God, not company directors or business managers. Before anyone chooses to undertake a pastoral ministry, they must settle the issue of which garment they are going to wear. If they are not willing to submit to being dressed contrary to their own preferences, they are heading for trouble. All selfish motives have to be removed before anyone can be a genuine pastor of God's sheep. Peter also had to learn to submit to the will of others. Being told what to do by others is something

---

127      Matt. 26:3
128      Acts 10:14

that many leaders find difficult. Strong-willed pastors can sometimes fail to detect the selfish motives directing their own ministry. When Pastors insist on dressing themselves, God will inevitably send someone along to call attention to their carnal behaviour. When the garments of Peter were not pure, God sent another apostle to address the issue.[129] This can be humbling to any leader, but all true pastors must also learn to be dressed by God and other leaders.

*John 21:7 'As soon as Simon Peter heard him say, "It is the Lord," he wrapped his outer garment around him (for he had taken it off) and jumped into the water.'*

Why had Peter taken off his garment? The answer to this question is linked to why he was fishing in Galilee when Jesus had told him to leave his boat and follow him.[130] These things give additional insight into the temperamental character of Peter. Despite leaving his fishing business, after things had not turned out as planned, Peter changed his mind about full-time ministry and declared, 'I'm going out to fish.'[131] In the process of asserting his own will to carry out actions not ordained by God, Peter removed his garment. The result was that no fish were caught despite

---

129     Gal. 2:11-14
130     Luke 5:11
131     John 21:3

a whole night of laborious effort. God will not grant success when his garment has been removed.

Whenever a leader decides upon a course of action without clear direction from God, they may lose their garment in the process. When there is no garment, there is no true success or lasting fruit. Only when Peter saw Jesus, did he realise his error. The first thing he did upon recognising the presence of his master, was to put his garment back on. He realised that he had become unclothed and needed to be appropriately dressed before meeting with God. In a purely natural sense, Peter's actions were very strange. Why would he put on his clothes to jump in the water? The reason can be seen in understanding the spiritual importance and necessity of the pastor's garment.

By returning to his fishing business when Jesus had called him away from it, Peter's disobedience unclothed him. It may have been to fulfil financial need or just because Peter wanted to do something that he felt he was good at. Many Pastors undertake similar enterprises today. Wanting to appear successful and affluent can often compete with the direct calling and instructions from God. Jesus had to reinstate Peter and remind him of his original calling. He was not to dress himself, but obey God.

*Acts 12:8 'The angel said to him "Put on your clothes and sandals." And*
*Peter did so. "Wrap your cloak around you."'*

In the twelfth chapter of Acts, Peter is again found unclothed. On this
occasion he is in the Jerusalem prison awaiting execution. Perhaps on
this occasion, Peter felt justified in taking off his pastoral clothes. He
had not chosen to be imprisoned and he was not seeking execution, so
he could have reasoned that his present predicament was not due, in any
part, to his own mistakes or selfish plans. He must have remembered
that his master told him he would suffer a martyr's death and, therefore,
assumed that his departure was imminent. His ministry appeared to be
over, so there did not seem to be any reason to wear his garment anymore.
As he lay asleep in apparent acceptance of his impending death, an angel
appeared in his cell and struck him on his side.

It was not, the end of his ministry and Peter was not going to die in that
prison. The angel had to violently wake the apostle and bring him to his
senses. Once fully awake, the angel gave him a very clear instruction -
get dressed!

Even in the midst of life's terrible situations, a minister must not take
off their garment. While a pastor is alive on earth, they have a ministry
to perform. They must never assume that their ministry is finished by

evaluating their immediate circumstances. Pastors can never fully retire, but must always be dressed ready for service.[132] Even though the circumstances appeared to show that his ministry was over, Peter was instructed to put his garment back on. Many pastors take off their garments because the church and denominational politics dictate that their ministry is no longer required. Some older servants of God may assume that, like Peter, they are left alone and overlooked with little prospect of any future ministry. They have forgotten, however, that God alone determines the end of a pastor's ministry. Until that time, they must remain robed even when a miracle is required to open the door of further ministry. God may perform the impossible, but only if his pastors remain clothed.


## *Paul*

*Acts 7:58 'The witnesses laid their clothes at the feet of a young man named Saul'*

The Apostle Paul was as born Saul of Tarsus and this proud Jew was born with the expectation of becoming a great leader. Since birth, he had been trained to be a teacher of men and a leading authority on the scriptures. His supreme knowledge and stubborn will would not bow to anyone's alternative interpretation of the scriptures. Nothing clothed this zealous

---

132      Luke 12:35

Pharisee more than his own pride. Full of his own self-importance as a 'Hebrew of Hebrew's,'[133] Saul expected other people's clothing be put at his feet as a sign of his superiority. People were subject to his direction and control and, therefore, their garments of service were to be placed under his authority.

All of this changed when he met the risen Lord on the road to Damascus. Saul would now have to become naked, repent and be baptised before he could be clothed with God's supreme garment of the Holy Spirit.[134] After his conversion he would become known as Paul, one of the greatest pastors in the early church. From his commission to pastor the gentiles, he always appeared to be ready and dressed to serve those he previously despised.


*2 Cor. 11:27 'I have been cold and naked'*

Throughout his ministry, despite much suffering, Paul continued steadfastly to the end. He was forced to be naked many times. He was often stripped before being flogged, stoned and beaten for the sake of the gospel. He also suffered shipwreck and had to swim naked in the open sea.[135] Despite every effort from his enemies to remove his garments,

---

133     Phil. 3:5
134     Acts 9:17-19
135     2 Cor. 11:23-25

Paul always got re-clothed and fulfilled his calling. Even when Agabus removed his clothing in a prophetic act of predicting his imprisonment and suffering, he still resolved to continue steadfastly in his ministry.[136] He knew that, because his garments were placed on him by God, no man could ever cause him to be naked again. He would continue to loyally fulfil his ministry to the end.

*Exd. 22:27 'His cloak is the only covering he has for his body. What else will he sleep in? When he cries out to me I will hear.'*

One of the worst aspects of Paul's ministry was not the persecution that he received from the world, but the abuse given to him by the church. This man who gave his life for the wellbeing of the church was often not appreciated by the very people who owed him their lives. Many pastors will go through similar experiences and will suffer mistreatment at the hands of the church. Everyone called to wear the pastor's garment will receive wounds in the house of their friends.[137] Nevertheless, Paul continued to serve the bride of Christ even when he was unappreciated and despised by her. Instead of supporting and helping with his ministry, some churches actively tried to remove Paul's ministry garment. They

---

136      Acts 21:13
137      Zech. 13:6

denied his true apostolic authority and viewed his preaching ability with contempt. Some claimed his teaching on grace promoted a sinful lifestyle[138] and even Peter acknowledged that some people purposefully distorted Paul's teaching.[139]

*Neh. 4:23 'neither I nor my brothers nor my men nor the guards with me took off our clothes'*

All of this lack of support could not remove Paul's pastoral mantle, and it should not affect leaders today. Although he taught that Pastors should receive payment from the churches they served,[140] when Paul and his team went without financial support they continued in their ministry calling and provided for their own financial needs.[141] Anyone wearing a genuine garment of a pastor will not withdraw his ministry when the salary is not lucrative. True servants of God are not hired hands greedy for money. While genuine pastors are not lusting after financial gain, churches must be clear about their own obligations. It is a disgraceful thing for a church to fail to look after its God-appointed ministers. A servant is worthy of his hire[142] and God will hear and act if his pastors suffer at the hands of

---

138     Rom. 3:8
139     2 Pet. 3:16
140     1 Cor. 9:14
141     1 Cor. 9:12
142     1 Tim. 5:18

the church. The body of Christ must ensure their pastors don't risk losing their garment due to financial hardship.

*2 Tim.4:6-13 'The time has come for my departure…bring the cloak I left with Carpus at Troas.'*

When Paul lay in the Roman prison writing to Timothy, he had completed over thirty years of pastoral and apostolic ministry. He knew that he was going to die and acknowledged that he was soon leaving to be with his Lord. It is worth noting the final requests of the apostle from his prison cell when facing imminent death. He could have, like Peter in Acts twelve, accepted his fate, laid down his ministry and succumbed to the impending martyrdom. Instead, he instructed Timothy to bring his garment. Peter took off his clothes when in a similar situation, but Paul wanted to put his garments on. As he told the Corinthian church, he always groaned to be clothed by God.[143] Paul understood the importance of the garment and he wanted to wear it to the end.

It is also important to note that he did not request any type of clothing, but specifically desired the cloak from Troas. This is important, because it was at Troas that Paul first had his vision and received his commission

---

143     2 Cor. 5:2

to leave Asia and launch his ministry into Europe.[144] It was at Troas that

Paul first wore the mantle of the Apostle to Europe. At the end of his life

on earth, Paul is found seeking to wear the garment that, reminded him of

the beginning of his European ministry. His shepherd heart still desired

to wear the pastor's garment to the very end. Paul continued to write and

shepherd the church during his final days on earth. Some of his greatest

advice came from his pastoral epistles, written in prison. Due to Paul's

faithfulness, the church is still being clothed by his pastoral words today.

---

144       Acts 16:8-10

# 9

---

# Clean Garments

*'Yet you have a few people in Sardis who have not soiled their clothes.*
*They will walk with me, dressed in white, for they are worthy.'*

### *Rev. 3:4*

*T*he church at Laodicea was naked, but did not know it. The church at Sardis was not naked, but had many members who were wearing dirty garments. Unclean clothes are not acceptable to God; his garment must always remain clean. The Christians at Sardis risked the possibility of being left behind when Jesus came 'like a thief,' because of the state of their clothing. The condition of believers' spiritual clothes is very important, as the scriptures make it abundantly clear that only those with clean garments can enter heaven. Every picture of the people that God accepts portrays them as wearing clean clothes.[145] When Jesus returns,

---

145        Rev. 19:8

those who are with him are still 'dressed in fine linen, white and clean.'[146]

Keeping one's clothes clean is an essential activity for every Christian. Anything that is unclean can never enter God's presence and every form of contamination must be avoided.

*Rev. 22:14 'Blessed are those who wash their robes, that they may have the right to the tree of life.'*

Only those whose garments are clean are granted access to eternal life. Seeing that this is so important, it is therefore essential for every Christian to grasp which things can soil their clothing, and how they can avoid them. It is not worth risking, even for a moment, anything that may defile or contaminate the precious clothing provided by Jesus. Each believer must take seriously the call to holy and clean living in order to prevent infection from the world.[147] Just as the apostle Jude instructed, every true child of God must hate 'even the clothing stained by corrupted flesh.'[148] Living a holy life is something that is rarely emphasised in modern Christianity. Some churches preach an unbalanced message of grace that deludes believers into thinking that God's mercy provides them with a free licence to live a sinful life. Such churches teach falsehood and

---

146      Rev. 19:14
147      James 1:27
148      Jude 1:25

deceive their members into thinking that their clothes of salvation will be kept clean, even if they roll around in the mud of the world. This kind of teaching perverts the true grace of God, which provided pure and holy garments for his children; clothes that he expects to be kept clean.

Things that defile the garments are too numerous to mention in great detail here. Violence, sexual immorality, drunkenness, filthy talk, deceit, jealousy, idolatry, discord, selfishness, envy and impurity are just some descriptions of the sinful nature outlined in scripture.[149] Any of these attributes of heart will make a believer's garment unclean. These things surround people on earth every day and can all too easily affect a believer in subtle measures. Fortunately, God has provided everyone with practical advice on how to keep their garments clean, even if they are assaulted by the sin that pervades the world.

*Num. 19:19 'The person being cleansed must wash his clothes and bathe with water, and that evening he will be clean.'*

God has provided an abundance of grace to enable everyone to keep their garments clean. He has supplied his pure water to wash the clothes that he has given to his children, so that they can be kept pure at all times. Water is very symbolic in the Bible and is often a picture of the cleansing

---

power of God.

Firstly, he has spoken about the water of his word.[150] God's word has a cleansing power that affects all who truly hear it. His word is spirit and life[151] and contains within it an ability to cleanse. By reading the bible or listening to the preaching of God's word, this powerful purifying effect will be bestowed upon those who have ears to hear. When Peter wanted to have a bath, Jesus said that he was already clean because he had believed his word.[152] Reading, reciting, hearing and meditating on God's word can cleanse a person's spirit, soul and body.

Secondly, God has provided an opportunity to repent. Initial Repentance was first enacted by water baptism where the water is a symbol of cleansing and purity. Although the sacrament of water baptism is carried out only once, repentance must continually occur in a Christian's life in order for their garments to be kept clean. Regular confession of sins is an essential aspect of God's cleansing process. Through the atoning blood of Christ, even guilty consciences can be kept pure and clean.[153] Repentance is not an optional extra in a believer's life and no one can be clean unless they turn away from all known sin. Everyone accepted by God has 'washed their robes and made them white in the blood of the

---

150     Eph. 5:26
151     John 6:63
152     John 15:3
153     Heb. 12:22

Lamb.'[154] Without genuine and constant repentance, many stains remain, spoil a believer's clothing and contaminates their walk with God.

Thirdly, Christians have access to the Holy Spirit. The Holy Spirit always cleanses and purifies everything he inhabits. Jesus said that the Spirit was a river of living water, and this eternal flow always keeps his garments clean. Being continually filled with the Spirit will prevent contamination, as he will powerfully wash away unclean substances from a believer's life.

*Lev. 13:47-49 'If any clothing is contaminated...it must be shown to the priest.'*

In the book of Leviticus, God gives a great deal of instruction about how to deal with unclean clothing. He goes into details concerning the type of contamination that may affect an article of clothing and how each garment is to be made clean again. The first thing to notice is that any stain on a garment had to be shown

*Any stain on a garment had to be shown to the priest. It must not be ignored.*

to the priest. It must not be ignored. This does not necessarily mean that all sin has to be confessed to a member of the clergy as all believers are

---

154        Rev. 7:14

now priests in God's sight. Many sins only need to be confessed to Jesus, the high priest; but no sin can be ignored. When sin affects a person's life, the worst thing they can do is ignore it and hope it will go away. This is a huge mistake, as sin is a deadly virus that grows and spreads if not treated. Only by recognising the blemish in the first instance, can the correct diagnosis be reached and the appropriate method of cleansing be administered.

*Lev. 13:53-53 'If, when the priest examines it, the mildew has not spread in the clothing, he shall order that the contaminated article be washed.'* When sin has been committed it must be confessed as soon as possible. Immediate recognition and repentance will prevent the contamination from spreading. One of the main reasons so many Christians are overtaken by sin, is because they fail to deal with small issues quickly, which results in the fault spreading further through their garment. If sins were examined whilst they were small it would prevent any drastic actions being taken in the future. The vast majority of sins start small and could be removed at an early stage. It is a sad aspect of church life that some sins spread through entire congregations before anyone attempts to deal with the issue. What starts out as a small indiscretion or simple gossip, can often multiply and cause hurt to the whole church. 'Consider what a great forest is set on fire by a small spark.'[155] If these sins were recognised and addressed in the beginning, the garment could be kept clean by the simple process of washing the problem away. Confessing God's word, acting in repentance and allowing the Holy Spirit to wash and cleanse the believer will result in the garment being free from blemish. Unfortunately, many people do not inspect the stain until it has spread, which means more drastic action has to be taken to make and keep the garment clean.

*Lev 13:56 'He is to tear the contaminated part out of the clothing.'*

Some sins are not confessed and, as a result, they grow. They soon develop into addictions and repetitive lapses in behaviour that can become destructive character faults. Unfortunately, many Christians fail to deal with issues in their infancy, which means the problems become harder to deal with as they grow. A stain that could have originally been eradicated by the process of washing, instead becomes stubbornly ingrained to such a degree that it cannot be removed.

God demands that our garments are clean and he will not tolerate sin. When his children fail to wash their clothes at the appropriate time, he has to insist that the stain is removed. His next course of action is to tear the blemish out of the clothing. Whilst this may seem severe, God

---

155      James 3:5

knows that the consequence of sin is death. If the issue is not dealt with, the virus will spread and pollute everything making the whole garment worthless. Jesus was very clear, if something would not be cleansed, it must be removed. 'If your right hand causes you to sin, cut it off and throw it away.'[156]

Tearing the garment was never God's original plan, as was seen in chapter four, but deadly sin requires emergency treatment. Many churches find this procedure difficult, but prolonging sinful activities only causes increased long-term damage. If bitter roots are allowed to grow, they will cause increased defilement.[157] It can be very painful to remove ministries and people that have become toxic, but it is often the only way to preserve the holiness and purity of the church. Cutting out activities from church programmes and removing certain individuals from ministry teams, however difficult in the short term, will result in purity later on. These individuals need not be totally lost, as God can sew the correct patch back on the garment afterwards, as long as the correct procedure has been followed.[158] Nevertheless, if the church fails to act when the garment becomes fully infected, then God has no alternative but to take increasingly severe action.

---

156     Matt. 5:30
157     Heb. 12:15
158     Luke 5:36

*Lev. 14:51 'if the mildew has spread on the clothing, or the woven or knitted material, or the leather, whatever its use, it is a destructive mildew; the article is unclean. He must burn up the clothing.'*

Some sins are so malevolent and destructive that washing and surgery will not remove them. Some people's garments have become so contaminated that they cannot be cleansed. When water will not cleanse something, fire will. Many Christians do not like to think that God judges by fire, but the Bible is clear that he does. Even John the Baptist, a prophet who was sent to wash with water, declared that Jesus would cleanse with fire.[159] God's first cleansing judgement on the world was with water, but his second judgement will be with fire.[160] Outside God's temple was a bronze basin where everyone who approached God could be cleansed.[161] In the Old Testament, those who despised obedience to God's commands, but still attempted to approach him, were often destroyed by fire.[162] In the New Testament, those who hate God and refuse to believe Jesus and be cleansed by the river of life, will face a lake of fire.[163]

The Christian's Garments must be kept clean in order to avoid more drastic procedures. The Apostle Paul instructed the Corinthian church

---

159     Matt. 3:11
160     2 Pet. 3:6-7
161     Exod. 30:18
162     Lev. 10:1-2
163     Rev. 21:8

that every ministry had to be tested and that, although individuals would be saved, some of their works would be burned up as worthless. Their garments were not clean.

*Acts 18:6 'He shook out his clothes in protest and said to them, 'Your blood be on your own heads!'*

To avoid the destruction by fire, every believer must avail themselves of God's procedures for keeping the garments clean. Even the dust must be shaken from the clothes of Christians. Dust is the food of the serpent[164] and the original material of man's old fallen nature.[165] No true believer wants their clothing contaminated by these materials. Whatever the attitude of the people of the world, every particle of dust from the old order of creation must be removed from the pure clothing of heaven.

---

164      Gen. 3:14
165      Gen. 2:7

# 10

## Worldly Garments

*I will punish…all those clad in foreign clothes.'*
### *Zeph. 1:8*

**D**espite God's provision of his wonderful spiritual garment, the temptation for Christians to adorn themselves in additional attire is very great. Although initially appreciating the value and beauty of the robes of Christ, many believers are soon tempted into laying aside their garments of righteousness in favour of wearing other clothes. They can all too easily be deceived into thinking that the garments of this world are tolerated by God and, once this lie is accepted, a different spiritual dress code is adhered to. Such people have failed to grasp that God will never allow his children to wear the garments of this world. They may appeal to the lust of the eyes, but God sees that they are improper robes, not meant to adorn his church, and he will continually warn his people to keep away from them. It angers him to see his people wearing the garments of this world. To abstain from the garment of the world does not mean that Christians should conform to some puritanical dress code in order to please God. The garment is not a literal item of clothing, but a picture of a believer's true spiritual condition.

*1 Pet. 3:3 'Your beauty should not come from outward adornment, such as...fine clothes.'*

Both Peter and Paul[166] stressed that a Christian's true worth did not come from the outward adornment of their worldly appearance. God has given his church something far more valuable than the visual aspects of clothing that appeal to the eyes. Despite the inward reality being stressed throughout the Bible, many churches still place most of their emphasis on how they appear outwardly. Enormous amounts of Christian resources are ploughed into outward visual enhancements aimed at placating the worldly appetites of church visitors. Such churches argue that the people of the world can only be reached by using the methods of the world. The result is that some places of worship are no different to bars or nightclubs, and even worse, many Christians' lifestyles are indistinguishable from unbelievers. This false logic of emphasising the outward apparel over

---

166        1 Tim. 2:9

the inner reality directly contradicts the clear teachings of scripture. It is also contradictory to the lifestyles of Jesus and his followers in the New Testament.

*Luke 16:19 'There was rich man who was dressed in purple and fine linen and lived in luxury every day. At his gate laid a beggar Lazarus.'*

The rich man wore worldly garments on earth but spent eternity in hell, Lazarus, on the other hand, wore simple clothes and entered heaven. The clothes that are worn in this story are a direct picture of a person's true inner condition and an indication of their future eternal destiny. It was highly unusual for a character to be named in a parable, which leads many to conclude that Lazarus may have been an actual disciple who was known by Jesus.

> *The rich man wore worldly garments on earth but spent eternity in hell.*

Jesus expected his disciples to always be recognisably different from the world. They were to be clothed in the Holy Spirit and not the garb of this life. There was a supernatural power that flowed from within their being and they were never instructed to strive to give an opulent outward impression. Everyone who met the apostles knew that there was something spiritually different about them.

Paul had his outward appearance described as 'unimpressive,'[167] but those same people could not deny the power that flowed from him.[168] The people that are hungry for reality are looking for truth, not outward displays. Christians must continue to wear the garment of God and not continually follow the latest Church trends that stress the improvement of outward adornment. The Laodicean church had outward beauty, but was naked before God. He has never been looking for an outward show, but true inner beauty. Concerning those who claim to belong to God but are merely putting on an outward show, the Bible says a day is coming when 'the Lord will snatch away their finery...the fine robes and the capes and cloaks.'[169]

The Kings of earth often force God's truly anointed leaders to parade in the garments of this world. These kings in the Bible expected the servants of God to be dressed appropriately for the kingdom they ruled over. Joseph was dressed as an Egyptian by Pharaoh,[170] Mordecai was robed as a Persian by Xerxes[171], and even Christ was mockingly clothed in purple by Rome.[172] Despite the attempts of these leaders to clothe God's anointed in their own garments, it did not affect their inner spiritual

---

| 167 | 2 Cor. 10:10 |
| 168 | 1 Cor. 2:4-5 |
| 169 | Isaiah 3:18-22 |
| 170 | Gen. 41:42 |
| 171 | Esther 6:10 |
| 172 | John 9:15 |

condition. Even when these world leaders claimed deity for themselves, and are metaphors of the Antichrist, God's men faithfully continued to serve the true God. They fulfilled the ministry they had been assigned, regardless of the fact that other people robed them in worldly majesty. A man's attitude to the garment of this world reveals the true inner desires of their heart. As can be seen in the lives of these famous people in the scriptures, the offer of a worldly robe reveals much concerning a man's genuine motives for service.

## *Daniel*

*Dan. 5:16 'If you can read this writing and tell me what it means, you will be clothed in purple.' Then Daniel answered the king "You may keep your gifts for yourself."'*

The Great prophet Daniel was tempted by the King to wear a Babylonian robe. This man of God would never succumb to such temptation, as he knew the futile vanity of such clothing. Daniel had encountered the man 'dressed in linen, with a belt of finest gold around his waist'[173] and he was not interested in wearing a worldly purple robe from Babylon; he was only going to wear the garment his Lord had given to him. Refusing to wear the Babylon clothing did not mean that Daniel refused to be successful

---

173      Dan. 10:5

in the world's affairs. On the contrary, Daniel was a highly successful individual in many spheres of life. He was a leading politician, a highly regarded prophet and he held several important official positions in the kingdom of Babylon. Despite his high profile success, however, Daniel never succumbed to the temptation of being dressed like the world. He always wore the garment of God.

The Babylonian robe is one of the great temptations Satan will present to Christians. He will attempt to trick them into believing that their abilities and gifting have also entitled them to be clothed in the outward glory of his kingdom, this world. He will offer genuine servants of God great wealth and luxury if only they will wear his clothes. It is a subtle and deadly trap into which many of God's servants have fallen. Having started out in simple faith wearing the clothing of their calling from God, many believers try to improve on what God has given them and dress to impress the world rather than their Lord.

No child of God must strive to wear the robe of Babylon. It is forbidden, and wearing it will cause great harm and destruction to every Christian's life.

## *Achan*

*Josh. 7:21 'When I saw in the plunder a beautiful robe from Babylonia...I coveted them and took them.'*

Where Daniel succeeded in resisting temptation, Achan failed. It is a very disappointing story, as his sin had disastrous implications for Achan's entire family and community. Everyone in Joshua's army had been given clear instructions that nothing could be taken from their victory of capturing Jericho. Achan knew that he was forbidden from helping himself to the Babylonian robe, which he found in the city, but he was unfaithful to his vows and his lustful heart gave into temptation.

What is sobering, is that Achan committed his sin after he achieved great victory. Some of the greatest temptations present themselves to God's people after they have achieved success. Perhaps Achan was humble before the battle of Jericho and would never have taken garment had he seen it in the desert. It could be that being one of Joshua's victorious soldiers, he felt entitled to wear his spoils of success, by wearing a robe from Babylon. He may have seen it as proof of his victorious ability and approval from God. He may have thought that being dressed in the world's splendour would bring him recognition and adoration from surrounding admirers. It is a very real truth that people can be humble whilst they are unsuccessful and unrecognised, but can't handle glory when they are triumphant in victory. 'Man is tested by the praise he receives.'[174]

Achan thought that he could hide his duplicity, but he was found out. God always knows which garment his children are seeking to wear. Defeat and destruction for his whole family were the consequences of his unfaithfulness. God will never bless anyone who wears the garment of this world, no matter how successful they may appear to have been in the past.

## Gideon

*Judges 8:27 'Gideon made the gold into an ephod...All Israel prostituted themselves by worshipping it...it became a snare to Gideon and his family.'*

Even great leaders can fall when it comes to the sin of wearing a worldly garment. In the four-hundred-year dispensation when the judges ruled the land, Gideon was one of its genuine and exemplary leaders. Nevertheless, even Gideon failed when it came to resisting the temptation of wearing the clothes of this world.

After his great victory in defeating the Midianites perhaps Gideon thought it was only a small matter to make an item of clothing for himself. After

---

174      Prov. 27:21

all it was not a full outfit but only a small ephod, just a token item of clothing to be worn as a symbol of his anointing and success. He may have even reasoned that it was a sign of God's approval. He had resisted the greater temptation of allowing the people to make him their king, but by making this small ephod would create huge problems.

When a leader allows sin into their life it will affect everyone around them. Gideon's ephod would be worshipped by those he led. Instead of enhancing true worship to God, it would become an idol to God's people. Once the false system of worship was accepted, a wrong priestly service would evolve and develop as a direct result of Gideon's wrong choice of clothing. As has been examined, a system of worship can always be evaluated by looking at the clothing of its priest.

### *False Priest*

*Judges 17:10 'Be my priest and I'll give you ten shekels of silver a year, your clothes and your food.'*

In the seventeenth chapter of Judges, a very strange story is told. It concerns a young Levite leaving his home in Bethlehem and taking a position as a priest in the land of Ephraim. There are many confusing aspects to this story, but some are clear indications that this young man was being disobedient to God. To start with, why was he leaving Bethlehem, the place that God had allocated to him for his ministry? Perhaps he did not believe the prophecies concerning the great things that would come out of Bethlehem and he wanted to live somewhere more exciting. Many people leave churches for the same reason today. They are bored where they are and don't believe what God has promised, so they refuse to be patient and hop from one church to another seeking something that will gratify their carnal desires.

The clearest indication of this Levite's reason for accepting this unauthorised position is that he would be provided with better clothing if he took the job. He was bribed by a man called Micah to take the role of priest. Being given clothing and a salary was sufficient for this man to relocate his ministry and be under the control of Micah, rather than the High Priest of Israel. Even when it became clear that the worship in Micah's house was not according to God's ordained pattern, as it involved the use of idols, it did not deter the Levite. His primary concern was to have money and be dressed as a priest. He would receive recognition because of the status that his clothing and title afforded him, and that was what he desired the most.

Jesus instructed all his ministers to not be concerned with money and clothing. Unfortunately, many leaders follow the example of the young

Levite rather that the instructions of God. Some of them relocate themselves in places that pay a good salary and give them a recognised title, rather than where God has specifically placed them. They love to wear the garment of the world and are prepared to make compromises, as long as they can keep their position and wear the clothes. There are many pastors belonging to churches and denominations who do not agree with many of the practices and beliefs of their institutions. Instead of taking a stand and refusing to compromise, they go along with things, against their consciences, because they want to wear the clothes and keep the title.

When ministers behave like this Levite, they are not genuine servants of God, but spiritual mercenaries and hired hands performing priestly service for the satisfaction of men. Such ministers cannot be trusted. They will always be looking for the next big thing that offers them greater prestige. When he received a better offer, the Levite again abandoned his position and moved north with the tribe of Dan. Once in his new location, wearing his false clothing, he implemented a false priestly system that continued for hundreds of years and corrupted and entire tribe and region.[175] A priestly system wearing false garments will always lead to the development of a church being dressed in the wrong robes.

---

175     Judges 18:31

## False church

*Rev. 17:3 'I saw a woman...covered with blasphemous names...The woman was dressed in purple.'*

When the worldly garment is worn by those in authority, the whole church soon becomes clothed inappropriately. A wrongly clothed priesthood results in a false church. False churches wear false clothing. Ultimately, the outcome of this error results in the Harlot dressed in purple at the end of the age, as described in the book of Revelation.[176] She is a picture of an entire religious system that is wrongly clothed and belongs to Satan's antichrist. It is essential that every believer is able to identify a false religious system and know the difference between this and the true church. A false church is easily identified by the clothing it wears.

Just like a priest, a false church is recognised by how it is dressed. A corrupt leader is motivated by money and a prostitute demands payment for her performance of love. Unfortunately, some churches act more like spiritual harlots than the bride of Christ. Believers must be aware of the spiritual clothing that adorns many places of worship that exist today. Any church that dresses in clothing other than that which God has provided, should be avoided. There are several aspects of a church's clothing that can be examined in order to discern whether it is a genuine house of God

---

176      Rev. 17:4

or a corrupt religious system.

*Psalm 73:6 'Pride is their necklace; they clothe themselves with violence.'*
Two aspects of a bad church are seen in its garments. Pride is always
sinful in an individual, but it can often be hidden when it is woven into
the very fabric of a church's clothing. Some churches can become very
proud of themselves and their achievements and become unaware of their
real spiritual condition. What can start out as encouragement and praise
concerning aspects of its own ministry, can develop into self-satisfied
pride in its own position. Legitimate ministries from God can be placed
upon pedestals, resulting in glory being given to groups of individuals
rather than to God. It was just like this in the time of Jesus, worshippers
were in awe of the temple buildings[177] and its adornments but failed to
recognise God in their midst.

Some Churches can become so proud of their musical abilities, equipment
or buildings that they spend most of their time engrossed in these external
aspects of service rather than being focused on God. Many people in
these organisations may not know the difference and think that they are
worshipping God, but they are idolising their own skills and performance
or their building decorations. Some congregations can become so

_____
177      Matt. 24:1

sophisticated in specific ministries that these secondary support services become all encompassing.

When engrossed in this deceived condition, Church services only become 'enjoyable' because of their state-of-the-art production techniques. Without noticing or being concerned, people lose focus and talk continuously about how awesome the design of the platform was or how brilliant the lighting and video effects were. While none of these things are wrong within a balanced context, many churches talk more about themselves and what they have achieved, than God himself. They end up wearing the pride of their own gifts, assets and abilities rather than God's garment.

Linked with pride, is the clothing of violence. Pride cannot tolerate opposition so anyone who criticises or questions the status quo is soon dealt with. This rarely takes the form of actual physical harm, but as Jesus said, violence resides in the heart. To discern the condition of someone's heart, you have to listen to their words, as 'the mouth speaks what the heart is full of.'[178] Anyone pointing out flaws in the church's clothing can be labelled as negative or ridiculed into silence. If someone dares to point out that too much attention is being placed on external issues, they are often treated as backward or old-fashioned. They can be labelled as

---

178      Luke 6:45

legalistic for wanting to focus on the simplicity of being clothed in the garment of God, rather than the trendy fashions of the world.

*Psalm 109:18 'He wore cursing as a garment.'*

An important aspect in recognising the clothing of a false church is by analysing what it says. Any pulpit that spends more time speaking against others than promoting the good news of God, may be wearing the wrong garment. A church should never curse others, as it has been called to bless. There are exceptional occasions where it is acceptable to pronounce a curse on things that are especially sinful,[179] but it should never be the regular garment that a Christian wears. Some churches are known more for what they hate than for what they love, which means they are probably wearing the wrong clothes. Jesus' greatest sermon is remembered for the things that he blessed, not the things that were cursed.[180]

*Psalm 23:21 'Drunkards and gluttons become poor, and drowsiness clothes them in rags.'*

An increasing number of churches appear to have abandoned the call to wear the garment of God and have settled for clothing made of rags.

---

179     Gal. 1:8-9
180     Matt. 5:3-11

By abusing the message of grace, many fellowships promote lifestyles that the Bible clearly condemns. This kind of excessive living results in the church being shabbily dressed, and it is becoming easier to spot. Undisciplined lives are a direct contradiction to the life Christ called his disciples to live. Spiritual laziness is rampant in the church during this present age. Spiritual disciplines are almost non-existent in the lives of some Churches. Whereas, the early Christians were very cautious in how they lived, including what they ate and drank, some churches advocate excessive styles of living that are inappropriate for Gods' people. His children were never meant to be clothed in rags.

This worldly clothing must be cast aside, just as Bartimaeus threw away his cloak used for begging.[181] Unfortunately, some churches will not reject the beggar's garment, they plead for money more than they ask for souls to be saved and healed. The true church is not clothed in rags, but the garment of God. Any Christian that has fallen into the error warned about by the apostle James by prioritising fine worldly garments instead of spiritual ones,[182] must change and be re-clothed. The garments of repentance are essential to bring people into a correct relationship with God.

---

181      Mark 10:50
182      James 2:2

# 11

## Garments of Repentance

*Rend you heart and not your garments.'*
***Joel 2:13***

*P*eople in the Bible would often tear their clothes as an outward sign of repentance. When confronted with wrongdoing, they could either ignore the rebuke, continuing to wear their own cloak of pride, or they could repent, tear off the clothes of sin and be re-clothed in the garment of God. When the worldly garment discussed in chapter ten is worn, it must be torn before the true clothing from God can be restored. True repentance that is accepted by God must reach the heart and must never be just an outward performance. The metaphor of the garment of repentance is only useful if it brings about true inner penitence and observable change in the wearer. All too often, people kneel at an altar or repeat a sinner's prayer without undergoing true repentance of heart concerning their sin. The garment of repentance is mentioned many times in scripture, but is primarily aimed at providing a picture of a true change of heart. Sometimes, it is the sinner who wears this garment, but often it is another advocate who repents on behalf of others. The true garment of God must never be torn but when worldly and selfish clothes of sin are genuinely ripped, or sackcloth is worn, then God can begin his glorious restoration process.

### Repentance for sin

*2 Kings 22:11 'When the king heard the words of the Book of the Law, he tore his robes.'*

Josiah was a good king who walked in the ways of God from a young age. Nevertheless, there came a day when the word of God was revealed to him in a way that he had never experienced before. Despite always seeking to obey God, the king became aware that his kingdom was living in direct rebellion against his commands. The nation had forsaken the Lord, indulged in idol worship and was serving false gods. Despite the King's best efforts and intentions, his people had discarded God's grace in order to wear the sinful garment of the world.

Josiah was so distressed at learning the truth from God's word that his heart was pierced with grief. Despite his Monarch's title and position, and the fact that he was wearing prestigious royal robes, his inner pain displayed an outward effect and he tore his robes in anguish. His repentance was real and everyone around him could see its outward demonstration. There was no allowance for royal pride or regal dignity, Josiah recognised that the wrath of a holy God was about to be unleashed on the unrighteous and unfaithful Kingdom of Judah, and he knew that they deserved the judgement that would come.

*2 Kings 22:19 'Because you tore your robes and wept in my presence, I have heard you, declares the LORD.'*

Josiah put on the garment of repentance just in time. Any delay in his penitence would have caused catastrophe for his entire generation. It is important to note exactly when Josiah tore his robe. His repentance occurred as soon as he heard God's word concerning the issue. His actions were immediate when he understood what God had really said about his condition and present situation. Whilst other leaders had ignored or twisted God's clear commands and instructions, Josiah fully realised that God meant what he said. In an age when many false teachers are changing God's written precepts, it is essential to hear and re-confirm the original statements of God, which do not change. Once heard, God's word must be acted upon immediately. Delay often proves fatal.

Too many people hear God's word concerning specific sins, but they defer action until a later date. They know that what they are doing is condemned by God, but they falsely assume that they can repent at their leisure at a more opportune time. This procrastination can prove deadly, as another opportunity is never guaranteed. The garment of repentance must be worn immediately upon hearing God's condemnation of any sin or lifestyle. Delay in appropriate action can result in a dullness of spiritual hearing that ends in someone becoming calloused and deaf to God's voice.[183]

Even the pagan king of Nineveh repented straightaway when he heard God's word of judgement over his sinful city, and he 'rose from his throne, took

> *The garment of repentance must be worn immediately upon hearing God's condemnation of any sin.*

off his royal robes, covered himself with sackcloth and sat down in the dust.'[184] This godless ruler of the Assyrians also commanded everyone in his city, including the animals, to be clothed in sackcloth.[185] His swift repentance before Jonah's forty-day deadline saved his city and his generation. Josiah's immediate action in tearing his garment also brought about forty years of protection for his people. Genuine repentance brings about true grace and forgiveness, but it must be authentic and according

---

183     Isa. 6:9-10
184     Jonah 3:6
185     Jonah 3:8

to God's commands, when sin has clearly been revealed.

## *Repentance for disobedience*

*Josh. 7:6 'Joshua tore his clothes and fell facedown.'*

Joshua had committed no personal sin, but he knew that a worldly garment had been brought into the camp that he led. Just like king Josiah, he was prepared to take responsibility for wrongdoing that had nothing to do with his own individual actions. Most leaders know that disobedience in their own lives cannot be tolerated by God, but many do not appear to fully grasp that sin in the church is also catastrophic and affects everyone in the camp, which leads to defeat for all. True ministers have to take the lead in wearing the garment of repentance, or the people will never follow their example. Some Pastors never appear to weep, fast or show pain of heart over the sin that affects the church. Jesus wept over the city that he loved when he knew the consequences of their sin.[186] Jesus wept at the tomb of Lazarus when he felt the pain of his friends mourning. He would have his outer cloak torn before being placed in his own tomb, when he atoned for the sins of the world.[187] Genuine leaders feel the inner pain when sin affects the flock that they lead, and it is often demonstrated in some form of outward display of emotion. They wear the garment of

---

186      Luke 19:41
187      John 19:23

repentance, even when it is on behalf of other people.

*Numb. 14:6 'Joshua son of Nun and Caleb son of Jephunneh...tore their clothes.'*

Being a true leader, Joshua was always prepared to take responsibility for situations, even when the problem did not originate with him. Like his Lord and namesake in the New Testament, Joshua never allowed his position to prohibit him from humbling himself for the benefit of others. In the above incident recorded in the book of Numbers, no actual physical sin had yet been committed, but the people were entertaining the sin of unbelief and were on the verge of rebelling against Moses and Aaron. Joshua understood that disobedience to God's appointed leaders was just as destructive as breaking his written commandments. He tore his garments to demonstrate the danger facing the people, who were intent on following their own opinions rather than God's faithful leaders. Unfortunately, the people failed to listen or to learn from Joshua's actions and did not repent or turn from their course of action. As a consequence of their unbelief, they spent forty years in a desert wilderness instead of flourishing in a land flowing with milk and honey.

Too many people fail to recognise the need to repent over making wrong decisions. Actions taken against the revealed will of God will always require repentance later on. The Christian world appears to be full of individuals who are organising their lives contrary to what God has planned for them, but because their actions are not outwardly sinful, they justify directing things according to their own choices and understanding. Many believers reject godly counsel and pastoral advice because they feel that their own opinion is equally valid, even when anointed leaders advise them against taking certain paths in life. There is always an unfortunate consequence to this course of action when it is contrary to God's will, and the garment of repentance must always be worn as a result.

## *Repentance for false exaltation*

*Acts 14:14 'When the apostles Barnabas and Paul heard of this, they tore their clothes.'*

The garments of repentance are not merely Old Testament metaphors, but are also worn in the New Testament. When the apostles visited the city of Lystra their campaign initially encountered evangelistic success when a man who was lame from birth was healed. Instead of giving glory to Jesus, in whose name the man had been healed, the crowd proclaimed that Paul and Barnabas were gods. The reaction of the apostles to being declared equal with deity, was to tear their clothes. They immediately recognised the great danger that had occurred. They knew that Herod himself had been struck dead when being declared a god by the crowd whilst 'wearing his royal robes,'[188] and they were not going to fall into a similar error. They would publically and outwardly repent from allowing the crowd to give them the glory for what God alone had done.

Paul and Barnabas display a sharp contrast from many so called apostles active in the church today. Instead of publically renouncing any glory coming from a crowd's adulation, many current high-profile ministers seem quite happy to wear as much glory as they can garner. Too many people think that they can amass glory for themselves whilst doing ministry for God. This can be especially noticeable in ministries that have a strong empowerment of supernatural gifting. Whilst being clothed with power is a good thing (Jesus himself said the Holy Spirit would do that)[189], clothing oneself in the glory reserved for deity is directly prohibited. God has clearly declared that, 'I will not yield my glory to another.'[190]

Often, articles can be published that exaggerate the abilities of God's ministers. The correct response for any individual when being afforded more glory than is warranted must be to publically repent from any embellished reports. A clear declaration must be made that God is the supplier of all supernatural life and power that all glory belongs to him.

---

188      Acts 12:21
189      Luke 24:49
190      Isa. 42:8

## *Sackcloth for society*

*Esther 4:1 'When Mordecai learned of all that had been done, he tore his clothes and put on sackcloth.'*

Mordecai had committed no sin against authority and neither had his people, the Jews. He is, however, found to be wearing the garment of sackcloth, not for himself or his people directly, but because he lived in a society that was passing unrighteous and unjust legislation. The Persian nation, in which he resided, had passed laws that would promote the persecution of God's people. The pain of this evil lawlessness pervading society affected Mordecai so intensely that he responded by wearing the garments of repentance. He hoped that God would see and act, and he would continue to wear the penitent robes until an answer came from heaven. Even when Queen Esther sent him better clothes to wear[191] and the king presented him with a royal robe,[192] Mordecai would not cease to cry out to God for mercy until righteousness was restored and his people protected.

---

191       Esth. 4:4
192       Esth. 6:10

*Joel 1:13 'Come, spend the night in sackcloth, you who minister before my God.'*

God is still seeking men and women of the calibre of Mordecai, people who will wear sackcloth on behalf of the society in which they reside. At a time of increasingly unjust legislation and unrighteous laws, God looks for those whose hearts are distressed at the sinful state of the nation around them. Too many people are seeking beautiful worldly attire, when the need of the hour is the sackcloth of intercession. David,[193] Hezekiah[194], and Isaiah[195] were just some of the great men of the Bible who spent seasons in sackcloth for the sake of the people around them. Due to their reverent submission, they were heard by God and their people were delivered. If society is not changed, then God's people become vulnerable to the culture encompassing them and often copy the behaviour of the world around them. The result can be that God's people succumb to the sin surrounding them and behave no different to the world.

---

193      1 Chron. 21:16
194      2 Kings 19:1
195      Isa. 20:2

*Ezra 9:3 'When I heard this, I tore my tunic and cloak.'*

Many of God's people had disobeyed God's commands during their seventy years in captivity and had 'mingled the holy race with the peoples around them.'[196] The children of God looked and behaved no differently from the people of the world. Ezra's response was to tear all his clothing. He was so appalled at their spiritual condition and the behaviour of the Jews that he was at a loss as to know what else to do. He knew that God would not accept a mingling between that which is holy and that which is unclean. Sadly, the condition and behaviour of some members of the church can also reach such low levels that leaders are too shell-shocked to know what to do. Divorce rates, abuse, legal disputes and immorality can often be worse in some churches than in the world around them. The response of leaders should be the same as Ezra and the great saints of the past. They should wear the garment of sackcloth and repentance and seek the mercy and grace of God. Only by believing in the gracious promise of receiving the beautiful garment of God can entice people to repent from the filth of the world. It is worth noting that Ezra was primarily concerned about the state of marriages of the Jewish people. This was because he understood the supreme importance of the marriage covenant in God's economy. The condition and function of the marriage sacrament

---

196      Ezra 9:2

in Christians is a key indicator of the general moral standard of a church. The principle of marriage is an essential component in understanding the importance of the garment of God. The garment of God is a wedding garment.

# 12

---

# Wedding Garments

*'When the king came in to see the guests, he noticed a man there who was not wearing wedding clothes.'*

**Matt. 22:11**

### Clothes for the guests

God has invited everyone to his great wedding banquet in heaven. In preparation for that great event, Jesus came to clothe everyone in his salvation, because God is not willing that any should perish.[197] Despite the fact that many are invited to join Jesus in heaven, it is nevertheless true that lots of people reject his invitation. It is also important to note that Jesus said that some will initially accept the invitation, but refuse to get properly dressed for the occasion. For someone to claim that they have come to God, while rejecting the very clothing that he offers, will result in the same punishment of an unbeliever. Those who have rejected God's wedding garment will be bound hand and foot and cast into the

---
197      2 Pet. 3:9

darkness.[198]

Only the garment of God is acceptable clothing for his wedding banquet. It is always easy to identify when people are dressed for a wedding, as their clothing speaks on their behalf. Everyone can see from their outward attire that they have dressed for a special occasion and prepared themselves to attend an important event. God's people know that they have accepted the invitation to belong to Christ and are preparing for the great celebration in heaven. They know that they must be clothed and ready for the 'wedding supper of the lamb.'[199] They would never jeopardise their highly favoured position by allowing their clothing to disqualify them from attending the occasion.

*Judges 14:10-12 'Samson made a feast there, as was customary for bridegrooms. "Let me tell you a riddle," Samson said to them. "If you can give me the answer...I will give you thirty linen garments and thirty sets of clothes."'*

It must be remembered that in Biblical times the bridegroom provided the wedding garments for the guests who were invited to his wedding. Many Christians may confuse aspects of Jesus' parable with the cultural

---

practices of today where the guests have to purchase, or manufacture, their own wedding clothes. The wedding garments of Christ can never be made by the efforts of man. Salvation is a gift from God and it can never be earned by the works of sinful man. Just like at Samson's wedding, so it will be at Christ's marriage banquet. The guests will only be clothed if they understand what the bridegroom is saying to them.

Samson was a flawed leader, but he still understood the importance of providing clothing for the people invited to his wedding. Jesus is the perfect bridegroom, so he will never fail to clothe his followers with the appropriate wedding garments.

*The wedding garments of Christ can never be made by the efforts of man.*

Nevertheless, the people invited still had to know what qualified them to wear the marriage clothes. Samson asked them all a question, and whether they would be provided with a garment was dependent upon their answer. His riddle was intended to ascertain whether they understood the nature of his recent victory over a ferocious lion.[200] If they did not know the answer, then they would not be properly clothed and could not attend the wedding.

Jesus' victory was far greater than anything that Samson achieved.

---

200      Judges 14:14-18

While the hero in the book of Judges killed an earthly beast, the son of God defeated the Devil who 'prowls around like a roaring lion looking for someone to devour.'[201] Christ destroyed the works of the devil[202], removed sin and conquered death. His victory was complete, perfect and everlasting. Through his salvation every fallen child of Adam and Eve can now be clothed with his salvation and attend his wedding celebration. What Jesus achieved on earth cannot be undone, and his accomplishment has now been ratified in Heaven by God the Father. Despite Christ's amazing victory, an essential question still remains. Just as Samson asked his guests for the answer, Jesus expects his followers to know how to obtain the wedding garment.

The clothing is obtained by confessing the victory of the bridegroom. The wedding garment is a gift that was won by Christ and there is no other way to wear it except by giving the correct confession and confirming that salvation only comes through faith in Jesus Christ.[203] In Jesus' parable, when asked where his garment was, 'The man was speechless.'[204] He had no answer because he did not truly know the master of the banquet. He had no acceptable confession of true faith and, consequently, was not clothed appropriately. A true child of God is never speechless concerning

---

201     1 Pet. 5:8
202     1 John 3:8
203     Rom. 10:9
204     Matt. 22:12

their salvation. They know they have been clothed by the salvation of Jesus Christ. They confess that he alone died for their sin and is now alive forevermore. They are now dressed ready for the wedding banquet that the king has arranged for all his invited guests.

*Luke 12:35-36 'Be dressed ready for service and keep your lamps burning, like men waiting for their master to return from a wedding banquet.'*

Jesus often linked the coming wedding banquet to the necessity of being clothed. Whenever the wedding supper is talked about in the Bible, a description of the guests' clothing is usually mentioned. This must be because wedding clothes are an essential requirement to being fully accepted by God. In the gospel of Matthew chapter twenty-five, Jesus gave his famous parable concerning his return. In this narrative about the virgin bridesmaids awaiting the approaching wedding, Jesus said that one day a cry will ring out, 'Here's the bridegroom!'[205] Bridesmaids are usually very meticulous in ensuring that everything is prepared for the special day - especially their wedding clothes - but in Jesus' parable only half of the virgins were ready for the wedding. They had accepted the invitation, but were not taken into the wedding reception. How embarrassing it would be if only half of God's people are ready for the

---

205      Matt 25:6

coming wedding when it arrives.

Even if some of the bridesmaids failed to be prepared, surely there is one individual at every wedding who is always wearing the correct clothing. Every marriage ceremony is empty and incomplete until the bride enters wearing her wedding garment.

*Deut 21:11-13 'If you notice among the captives a beautiful woman and are attracted to her...put aside the clothes she was wearing when captured...and she shall be your wife.'*

In the Law of Moses, the Israelites were allowed to marry women who may have previously been seen as enemies and slaves. It is amazing to notice that even before Christ demonstrated his love for his Bride on the cross, God had already made provision in the Old Testament concerning acceptable marriage clothes. God has always been planning to prepare a Bride that is acceptable for his son. Even if she had previously been a slave to sin, an enemy of all that is good and unclean in her lifestyle, she could still be chosen and accepted as a bride. Before this could be considered, however, her old clothes had to be discarded. They were not appropriate for a bride on her wedding day. Once the sinful garments were removed, the woman was ready to be dressed with the clothing of a bride. The book of Exodus made it clear that all husbands had to provide their wives with acceptable clothing.[206] If God commanded earthly husbands to clothe their wives correctly, how much more beautifully will the Bride of Christ be dressed for her wedding?

### *The Bride's Garment*

*Rev. 21:2 'I saw the Holy City, the New Jerusalem, coming down out of heaven from God, prepared as a bride beautifully dressed for her husband.'*

At the end of the Bible, John described God's people as a bride dressed for her husband. Throughout the scriptures, the bride is a metaphor for God's people and her clothing is essential in correctly identifying her. At a wedding it is easy to spot the bride, as she is dressed differently from everybody else, likewise, God's people are recognised by the spiritual clothing that they wear. If a church is truly a part of the bride of Christ, then she will wear the same clothes as described in the book of Revelation.

*Rev. 19:7-8 'The wedding of the lamb has come and his bride has made herself ready. Fine linen, bright and clean was given her to wear.'*

Every true bride wants to wear the best wedding dress for her special day. When Jesus comes for His church, she will be recognised by the

---

206        Exod. 21:10

clothes she wears. Isaac recognised his future wife Rebekah when she first approached him, because she was wearing the clothes that he had sent her as a gift.[207] If any church fails to be clothed in the garments that God has provided, they risk missing the wedding reception, just like the undressed bride in the Song of Songs.[208] She failed to wear her correct clothing when her bridegroom came for her and was left behind when he departed. The church also must wear the correct clothing if it is to be accepted as the bride of Christ and taken to be with the king.

*Psalm 45:14 'In embroidered garments she is led to the king.'*

The wedding dress of God's people has very specific aspects to it. Firstly, it is fine linen, which 'stands for the righteous acts of the saints.'[209] It has been seen in other chapters that linen clothing represents many aspects in a believer's life and it is also essential that a church's robe is of the same holy material. In John's vision, the wedding garment is made of the good deeds of God's people. The primary duty of every church is to fulfil the role of the linen robed priests. Whilst the church is preparing to attend a wedding celebration in heaven, it also has an essential duty and role to fulfil on earth. Worship, prayer, study of God's word, serving and

---

207      Gen. 24:53
208      Song. 5:3
209      Rev. 19:8

reaching out to others are all key components of the life of every true church. Failure to carry out the bridegroom's commands will result in inappropriate clothing being worn and possible rejection at the banquet. If a church has no righteous deeds, it cannot hope to be dressed correctly for the wedding.

*Psalm 45:13 'Her gown is interwoven with gold.'*

Secondly, the wedding dress is shining. Not only is the linen bright and clean, but the gold in the garment reflects the glory of God. Just as Christ's garment shone with a heavenly brightness,[210] so his bride's garment must also glimmer with God's glory. The golden fabric inside God's temple was not usually seen by ordinary people, just like Christ's glory was often hidden from the world. Although unappreciated by many, the shining radiance of God was still present in his temple. In a similar way, the church's beauty is usually overlooked by society, but it must still be present nonetheless. If any church does not have the glory of the presence of God shining from within, it is heading for trouble. This does not mean it has to have the best music or building decorations, but God's church is a golden lampstand[211] from which brightness is meant to

---

210      Matt. 17:2
211      Rev. 1:20

shine. The bride's lamp must always shine with the brightness of God, her lamp must not go out at night[212] and she must never run out of oil.[213] If a church's garments are not bright, some aspect of the fabric is missing and there is a serious problem with her gown.

*Rev. 7:14 'They have washed their robes and made them white in the blood of the Lamb.'*

Thirdly, the bride's clothes are clean; they are spotless. Everything about the bride of Christ is clean, especially her garments. Today, too many Christians excuse dirty habits thinking that they will not affect their condition before God, but only those who are clean can approach him[214]. In the scriptures brides were always cosmetically prepared before their wedding day[215],as all good husbands love their wives cleansing them 'by the washing with water through the word.'[216] Likewise, Jesus has washed his bride, so that she is 'without stain or wrinkle or any other blemish'[217] and he expects her to stay clean. No woman wants her dress to be soiled on her wedding day, and no genuine believer wants to appear at the marriage supper of the lamb in dirty clothes. All sin must be confessed and washed

---

212     Prov. 31:18
213     Matt. 25:8
214     Psalm 24:3-4
215     Esth. 2:12
216     Eph. 5:26
217     Eph. 5:27

away from a Christian's life before the wedding. Despite many people falsely claiming that grace gives them an excuse to remain dirty, no one should risk wearing dirty clothes and be ejected from the ceremony.

*Ruth 3:3 'Wash and perfume yourself, and put on your best clothes.'*

When Ruth desired to become Boaz's bride she had to first put on her best clothes. Before he would 'spread the corner of his garment'[218] over Ruth, she had to be dressed correctly. All brides must wear their best robes if they are to be accepted by the bridegroom. Ordinary daily clothes are not good enough to wear to the wedding. Today, many people don't give God their best. They think that any level of service or devotion to him will be accepted, but Jesus said that we have to love the Lord with everything that is available.[219] Only the best clothes are acceptable for the bride to wear and all Christians must give their best to God if they desire to be taken into the wedding.

When she wears her best clothes, the bridegroom is always willing to listen and assist his bride. When Esther wore her most valued robes, her king and bridegroom accepted her and granted her petitions.[220] When the church puts on her bridal robes, God is also ready to listen to her prayers

---

218     Ruth 3:9
219     Mark 12:30
220     Esth. 5:1-3

and grant her requests. He never fails to answer his beloved when she is robed in his purity and righteousness.

## *Prostitute's Clothes?*

*Prov. 7:10 'Out came a woman to meet him, dressed like a prostitute.'*

There is a huge difference between the clothing of a prostitute and the garments of a bride. There is also a massive difference between a true church and a false one. The false church has already been examined in the chapter on worldly garments, but it must be remembered that even a good church can soon allow its clothes to become tainted. A bride dresses for love, but a harlot is clothed for hire and to make a profit. She is dressed to entice and appeal to the carnal lusts of sinful men.

Ministries that were once performed out of love and devotion to God can often descend into routine professionalism. Pastors that once served God's flock out of genuine care and concern may fall into the trap of becoming a hireling for money. Once deluded into this line of self-seeking, ministries can descend into appealing to the carnal desires of people in order to achieve their financial or egotistical needs. They preach what will satisfy man's desires instead of what pleases God. They end up dressing the church like a harlot rather than a bride. To the prostitute in the book of Revelation, the fine linen garments were just commodities to be traded.[221] Greed and control were the motives for her actions, not love. The dangers are very real. A powerful guard against falling into such error is a continual examination of the clothes that are worn by the church. Is the ministry that is being provided pleasing to God? Would it be acceptable on the great wedding day when Christ returns? The church must never dress as a prostitute, as the harlot's final condition is to be stripped naked and destroyed.[222] Ezekiel describes the process of stripping an unfaithful bride in graphic detail.[223] The church is not a prostitute but God's bride and she is being dressed in her wedding garment. It is clothing appropriate for her wedding, as described in chapter nineteen of the book of Revelation. What is astounding is that the wedding clothes appear identical to the battle garments worn by those following Jesus Christ when he returns to earth. Christ's Bride is not merely dressed for beauty; she is also dressed for battle.

---

221     Rev. 18:12
222     Rev. 17:16
223     Ezek. 16

# 13

## Battle Garments

*'He is dressed in a robe dipped in blood...On his robe and on his thigh he has this name written: KING OF KINGS AND LORD OF LORDS.'*
### Rev. 19:13-16

*W*hen Christ returns to earth, specific attention is focused on the clothes he wears. He is returning as a warrior prepared for battle. Hundreds of years earlier, Isaiah also prophesied that he saw the same 'blood spattered'[224] clothing being worn by the coming Messiah. The prophets not only saw Jesus clothed as a prophet, priest, and king, they also saw him robed as a warrior who will unleash his vengeance on all evil and iniquity that refuses to believe the truth. On that day, he will 'put on the garments of vengeance and wrap himself in zeal as in a cloak.'[225] When Christ comes again, however, he does not come alone. Riding with him is a vast company of people that no man can number. The Bible does not

224     Isa. 63:1-3
225     Isa. 59:17

inform us of their names but it does tell us what they are wearing. They are an army clothed in battle garments

*Rev. 19:14 'The armies of heaven were following him, dressed in fine linen, white and clean.'*

At Christ's return those who accompany him are wearing the garments of God. These saints are riding into battle and the armies of God are clothed appropriately, as the garment of God is also the armour of God. Heaven's clothing is often described as armour in the Bible. If a Christian fails to be clothed in God's protective body armour, they will soon fall

> *No flame of the evil one can penetrate the protective power of the armour of God.*

under the constant assault from the evil that surrounds them. Satan's evil accusations are routinely being fired at God's children, but if they wear the correct armour of God they can 'extinguish all the flaming arrows of the evil one.'[226] However intense the conflict, believers are protected when they are wearing the armour of God; the Devil's fire cannot touch them. The three faithful youths in Daniel's story provide a wonderful illustration of the protection afforded by wearing the clothing of God. Although they

---

226      Eph. 6:16

were viciously assaulted by the agents of Satan, they were protected in the midst of the fire. After their ordeal in the furnace 'their robes were not scorched, and there was no smell of fire on them.'[227] No flame of the evil one can penetrate the protective power of the armour of God.

*Eph.6:13-14 'Put on the full armour of God...with the belt of truth buckled around your waist, with the breast plate of righteousness in place.'*

The importance of the belt has already been considered but the link between the belt and the breastplate needs to be emphasised. The belt represents truth, whereas the breast plate is a picture of righteousness. Unless God declares a person righteous, they have no hope in this world and they will fall in battle at the first accusation. It is only by wearing God's righteousness that anyone can be saved. This breastplate guards the heart from the accusing and condemning darts of the Devil. He continually slanders God's people by claiming that they are unrighteous due to their sins and faults. When a Christian wears the breastplate, Satan's arrows of accusation cannot penetrate into the heart and condemn the child of God. They are declared righteous through their faith in Christ, as they wear his clothing. Most Christians understand this concept and accept that they

---

227      Dan. 3:29

are saved through the righteousness of Christ,[228] never through their own goodness, and they now receive his protection and readily wear his body armour.

*Isa. 59:17 'He put on righteousness as his breastplate.'*

It is unfortunate that some Christians forget that they are told to put on the full armour of God, not merely the breastplate. There is no protection unless there is genuine obedience. When a roman soldier dressed for battle, he would first put on his belt, because from his belt would hang the rest of his armour. His breast plate would hang over his chest, because it was suspended and held in place by leather straps that hung over the shoulders and were fastened to his belt. In other words, if the belt is not worn then the rest of the armour will not stay in place.

If a Christian refuses to wear the belt of truth, then their righteousness will fall to the ground and they will have no protection against evil accusation. Unfortunately, many believers claim to wear the righteousness of God while refusing to accept his complete truth. They falsely believe that they can accept the grace of God's righteousness, when refusing to live by his truth. This is a serious error that will prove catastrophic for any child of God to believe. The full armour must be worn, and this includes living by

---

228      Titus 3:5

God's truth as well as claiming to be saved by his righteousness.

Too many people are claiming to follow Christ, but are not living by the truth. These deceived individuals believe the lie that they can be accepted by God whilst denying his clearly stated truths. The moral relativism of the world has no place in the lives of God's people. God has written that specific activities and lifestyles are wrong and he will not change his mind on these stated commands. If anyone has removed these truths from their lives and rejected God's moral standards, then they also forfeit the right to claim God's righteousness, which will result in their condemnation.

## Mark 6:8 'Take no money in your belts'

The truth must remain untainted from this world's corruption and should never be twisted to accommodate popular opinion or be manipulated for selfish gain. Soldiers who serve in God's army must never use their position to obtain unauthorised perks of the job. Their uniforms give them authority in fighting God's battles, but not the right to extort anything for personal gain. John the Baptist clearly warned soldiers not to 'extort money' and to 'be content with your pay.'[229] Jesus instructed his disciples that they must have no 'gold, or silver, or copper' in their

---

229     Luke 3:14

belts.[230] It is not merely those who minister for the opulent lifestyle of gold that are condemned, but also those who seek the lesser selfish gains of silver and copper. Carnal desire and selfish ambition are always judged as evil practices by God.[231] The belt of truth must remain pure from selfish corruption or the breastplate of righteousness will fall to the ground. To preach the truth for personal prestige or worldly riches will always compromise a Christian's righteousness and 'stain the belt around his waist.'[232]


## Satan's Armour

*1 Sam. 17:4-5 'Goliath…wore a coat of scale armour of bronze weighing five thousand shekels.'*

When Goliath came out to defy the living God and challenge his people, the Bible gives a detailed description of the giant's armour. His armour weighed about one hundred and twenty-five pounds, not including his helmet, greaves and carrying weapons.[233] No Israelite soldier was prepared to confront Goliath in combat, as his armour was considered impregnable. Goliath was six cubits in height, had six items of battle equipment, with a spear point weighing six hundred shekels. Whenever

---

| 230 | Matt. 10:9. |
| 231 | James 3:16 |
| 232 | 1 Kings 2:5 |
| 233 | 1 Sam. 17:5-7 |

someone is identified by the number 666 in the Bible, he is a picture of

Satan's champion, preparing to destroy God's people.[234] Just as this evil

giant from Gath boasted that he was too strong to be defeated by the true

God, Satan makes similar taunts to Christians in this present age.

The devil's tactics have not changed over the course of human history.

His proud pronouncements of his invincibility have echoed throughout

the ages. The ancient serpent continues to make his challenge of, 'who

can strip off his outer coat?' and stating that, 'his back has rows of shields

tightly sealed together.' He says that any sword that reaches him has no

effect, nor does the spear or the dart or the javelin.[235] He boasts that his

armour is greater than anything worn by God's people. He declares that

in his armour he is invincible and can never be defeated by the weak and

feeble church.

Satan's armour is reinforced by the perpetual lies of fallen humanity.

He claims that through science, knowledge, philosophy, politics and

humanistic rationalism, he cannot be overcome by the simple and childish

belief in Jesus. Upon hearing these complicated, articulate and proud

statements, many believers are terrified, just as Saul's soldiers cowered

behind their shields when confronted by Goliath. They reason that they

---

234      Rev. 13:18
235      Job 41:13-30

are unequipped to fight the enemy due to their lack of ability against his considerable might. Some may even feel that human secularism and false religions have already won the battle against the church of Jesus Christ. Many churches have already admitted defeat, refused to fight and capitulated against the onslaught of Satan's lies. The truth, however, is that Satan is a liar. Whilst his armour was indeed very powerful, there was someone who wore a more powerful garment when confronting him in battle. Satan's armour is no match for anyone wearing the garment of God.

*Luke 11:22 'When someone stronger attacks and overpowers him, he takes away the armour in which the man trusted.'*

Just as David defeated Goliath, in spite of his strong armour, a greater warrior from David's family would conquer Satan forever. When Christ defeated death and sin at the cross, he also stripped Satan of all his armour. The Devil continues to bully and intimidate the church with the lie that it is powerless against him, but his deceit does not work on those who know the truth. When Satan stripped Jesus at the cross, little did he know that within three days all of his proud armour would be removed forever. When the Pharisees claimed that Jesus operated by the power of Satan, Christ's answer was that he drove out devils by the power of God.[236] He made it clear that he was here to defeat Beelzebub and strip him of all his armour.

Christians must always rely on Christ's victory when in conflict with evil, and must not be intimidated by Satan's proud boasts of impregnability. The armour of man's humanistic world has been removed. Believers know that Christ's resurrection destroyed all the power of the enemy. They must stand in the victory of Christ's garments and never fall into the temptation of wearing the armour of man or this world.


## Man's Armour

*1 Sam. 17:38 'Saul dressed David in his own tunic. He put a coat of armour on him.'*

Despite his considerable armour, Goliath was no match for David because this simple shepherd boy was clothed in the anointing of God. It must be noted, however, that before the giant was engaged in combat, another piece of clothing was placed on David. He was presented with an alternative garment in which to place his trust, instead of total reliance on his anointing from God. Every believer will likewise be presented with the option of wearing this piece of armour in addition to the protection of

---

236      Luke 11:20

God's clothing. This temptation must be firmly resisted.

This armour belonged to Saul. It was the battle garment of the rejected king and the clothing of fallen man and leadership that lacked anointing. It looked strong, reliable and necessary in the eyes of men, but it conveyed no power from God and it was powerless to help David. Saul was man's opinion of what was required to succeed in serving God. He was chosen by men,[237] acceptable in appearance to human appetites[238] and was skilled at being a people-pleaser.[239] He wanted to be seen as helping David, but he had no real desire for him to succeed as he was only concerned about enhancing his own status. He wanted to be able to claim the credit for any victory that was won and thrived on being acknowledged as the strongest and most anointed leader in the land.

It is a sad indictment on the state of leadership when pastors are more concerned with keeping their own position, title and status than with God's people obtaining victory. He would allow David to have victory only upon the condition that he did it looking like Saul and using his approved methods. David, however, was already wearing armour that Saul no longer perceived nor understood. David was covered in the anointing of the Holy Spirit and was wearing the garment of God. Man's

---

237     1 Sam. 10:19
238     1 Sam. 10:23
239     1 Sam. 15:24

clothing would be of no benefit to him and he could not place any trust in it. He refused to conform to an old system of un-anointed leadership that adhered to a mere outward appearance of acceptability. Instead, David chose to place his total trust in the God who clothed him in the protective covering of his Holy Spirit. In doing so, Goliath's armour was no protection from God's anointed and David's victory was assured.

*1 Kings 22:34 'Someone drew his bow at random and hit the king of Israel between the sections of his armour.'*

If anyone wears the armour of carnal leadership, they will always be hit by the arrows of the enemy. King Ahab was a fallen leader like Saul and he likewise died in battle despite wearing his armour. Man's armour, however impressive to ordinary eyes, is no protection against an evil attack.

David was expected to wear Saul's armour, because carnal people demand that God's leaders conform to their own opinion of acceptable appearance and behaviour. To fight the giants of this secular and humanistic world, people believe that they must be clothed like Goliath and trust in man's abilities. They reason that for a leader to defeat the world in its considerable armour, they must also be equipped in the same clothing. They often insist that ministers are highly educated in the philosophy and politics of the world and expect them to have understanding and experience in its arts and activities. It is assumed they must first have studied high levels of theology and biblical criticism before they are equipped to serve God. And they may believe denominational traditions must be adhered to as well as ecclesiastical calendars and practices. Bible colleges and seminaries churn out the next generation of ministers who are clothed in academic practices and abilities, but often know nothing of simple faith in God's anointing. Like David, believers must learn to put their trust in God's armour instead of man's. If they fail to do so they may become like Saul, a leader with a title but no anointing, hiding behind his outward achievements, but never winning any real victories. They could end up clothed only in human wisdom and lacking in God's armour.

*1 Sam. 18:4 'Jonathan took off the robe he was wearing and gave it to David, along with his tunic, and even his sword, his bow and his belt.'*
While David rejected Saul's armour before the conflict, he accepted Jonathan's battle garments after he had obtained victory. He would not rely on human ability instead of God, but that did not mean he rejected genuine friendship and help from other anointed people. Although believers must never replace God's battle garments with carnal abilities, they should always be open to receiving benefits from brethren who

are also anointed, but in different ways. David first proved his faith by trusting in God's protection rather than man's clothing, but afterwards he was prepared to put on the battledress of his best friend. While this could appear to be a contradiction at first glance, reliance on God's armour should never become an excuse for dismissing other Christians whom God has anointed and blessed in different ways and with specialised garments. God does command some of his children to be highly educated and work in the politics, philosophies and systems of this fallen world, even though others gain their self-reliance and prestige from such positions.

Although the wrong armour must always be removed before any spiritual conflict, believers must ensure that they wear God's battle garment at all times. Every true child of God must 'put on the armour of light'[240] that has been given to them, so that they will be protected and victorious in all he has called them to achieve.

240    Rom. 13:12

# 14

---

## The Garment of God

*'Clothe yourself in the Lord Jesus Christ'*
### Rom. 13:14

**W**hen a believer wears the garment of God, they are clothed with Jesus himself. Whilst this may sound a strange concept, it must always be remembered that every positive aspect of the garment mentioned in this book is only a metaphor of the reality that is contained in Christ himself. God's clothing always points towards the unique attributes of Jesus. His clothing was always a parable to those who were genuinely looking to God and listening to what he was saying. Even when he was born, the shepherds would recognise the Son of God by the clothing he wore. The angels told them 'this will be a sign to you: You will find a baby wrapped in cloths.'[241] The clothing of Jesus was always a sign of who he was and

---

241      Luke 2:12

what he had come to do. He wore the garment of God at his birth and throughout his ministry, until it was removed at the cross. When Christ was raised from the dead, just like Lazarus, the grave clothes of death were left at the tomb.[242] In heaven, he now wears a robe of majesty and splendour.[243] Now that he is glorified, he gives believers his garment so that they can be covered by his mantle and perform the works that he did. When God's garment is worn, a Christian is empowered to do the same things that Jesus did.[244] Just as the clothes of Jesus were living parables that illustrated his ministry on earth, so God desires to likewise clothe his children during their pilgrimage through this world. If Christians will wear the clothing described in the previous chapters and appropriate its essential meaning, then it will produce similar effects that were observed by Christ's garments.

### Garment of Power

*Luke 24:49 'I am going to send you what my father has promised; but stay in the city until you have been clothed with power from on high.'*

The garment of God provides the wearer with a covering of power. The Father and the Son have instructed believers to wait until they have

---

242     John 11:44 & 20:6
243     Rev. 1:13
244     John 14:12

been clothed with the power of the Holy Spirit before moving forward in mission and ministry.[245] Jesus waited until he was clothed with the Holy Spirit before beginning his ministry and the Apostles also tarried until they were endued with the power from on high.[246] Paul stressed that churches must understand that, 'all of you who were baptised into Christ have clothed yourselves with Christ.'[247] The baptism of the Holy Spirit is not merely a doctrine to accept in the mind, it is an experience that covers believers with

*To proceed into ministry before putting on the garment, will result in absence of the supernatural power.*

clothing that must be worn. The Holy Spirit cannot be reserved for special occasions like some people use their best attire; He must be worn at all times. It is essential that all Christians put on the power of the Holy Spirit before attempting to succeed in their God appointed mission. To proceed into ministry before putting on the garment, will result in absence of the supernatural power that is necessary for the mission.

The power in Christ's garments manifested itself in many different ways. The Holy Spirit will also distribute his power in manifold ways once he

---

245     Mark 1:10
246     Acts 2:1-4
247     Gal. 3:27

has clothed his people. The gifts and the fruit of the Holy Spirit can be identified and described in a variety of ways and each attribute is valuable, but the most precious aspect is the clothing itself, the very presence of God on a person's life. From this garment flows all the power of God.

### Garment of Healing

*Mat 14:35-36 'People brought all their sick to him and begged him to let the sick just touch the edge of his cloak, and all who touched it were healed.'*

Although Jesus proclaimed that he had come to heal the sick,[248] he never actually told the crowds that his clothing would heal people. The multitudes grasped intuitively that there was a unique power resting on Jesus, in the same way that a garment covered a person. They knew that although Jesus was a man with flesh and blood, he was nevertheless clothed in the supernatural Spirit of God and this power would be released if they touched his cloak.[249] They would have read about Moses who had leprosy healed when it was placed inside his cloak and they could see that a greater saviour was now present amongst the people of Israel. Perhaps the crowds had heard the testimony from the woman in

---

248      Luke 4:18
249      Exod. 4:6

Capernaum who had been healed from her disease when she touched the hem of his garment.[250] It may be that once one person had experienced healing from the power present in the clothing of Christ, that many other sick people would copy her faith and receive their own miracle.

Touching Christ's clothing was not a superstitious activity of the people of Galilee. The Holy Spirit was genuinely covering Jesus and all who recognised this, by faith, could gain access to the same power. It was not only Christ's clothing that possessed the power to heal. The Apostles who were filled with the same Holy Spirit would continue to do the same works of Jesus. Paul's clothing also contained healing power.[251] This was not because of any undue religious sacramentalism, but because people recognised that the Spirit of healing power rested on the apostle, just as it had the Son of God. The same Holy Spirit clothes his disciples today, so that healing flowing from the garment resting upon them can give power to others.

---

250      Matt. 9:21
251      Acts 19:11

## *Garment of Glory*

*Mark 9:2 'There he was transfigured before them. His clothes became dazzling white, whiter than anyone in the world could bleach them.'*

On the mountain of transfiguration, the disciples saw the manifest glory of God revealed through the garment that Jesus wore. Luke said, 'his clothes became as bright as a flash of lightning'[252] and Matthew said they 'became as white as the light.'[253] All the gospel writers called attention to the fact that it was the clothing of Jesus that revealed the glory of God. The purity of the clothes was emphasised in their brightness being greater than anything in this world. They were filled with something that came from the heavenly realm, like lightning, like the essence of light itself. Of course, the true glory of God is indescribable and cannot be contained by the mere words of men. There is no earthly language that can adequately describe it, but whilst it cannot be articulated, it can still be worn.

On that holy mountain, the apostles glimpsed the mysterious glory and power of the garment of God. It was beyond their comprehension, something too glorious to behold with their limited natural senses. Had they understood the scriptures, they would have fully grasped who now stood before them, as God himself is robed in light.[254] Despite the

---

252      Luke 9:29
253      Matt. 17:2
254      Psalm 104:2

limitations of human understanding, they knew that the clothes of Jesus were changed from their natural appearance to reveal their real spiritual condition. The Holy Spirit likewise transforms all those who are clothed by him. They are changed from a merely natural condition into a heavenly disposition. The garment of God continues to transform them from 'glory into glory'[255] as long as they remain clothed in his presence.

The three disciples on the mountain were privileged to observe the true nature of the garment of God, whilst everyone else down in the valley only saw the earthly outward appearance of the clothes of Jesus. Most people on earth failed to recognise the mantle that covered the son of God as he walked the hills of Galilee. What was the experience of the Son of God, will also be true for his disciples. Many will never accept the truth and glory that robes the children of God, as it is hidden from their carnal eyesight, but the clothing of the Holy Spirit shines and transforms genuine Christians as they abide under his covering.

---

255      2 Cor. 3:18

## *Garment of sacrifice*

*Matt 5:40 'If anyone wants to sue you and take your shirt, hand over your cloak as well.'*

Jesus did not merely teach about wearing the garment of God, he demonstrated it throughout his life and ministry. He made it very clear that wearing the mantle of God obligated the wearer to live a life of sacrifice. Jesus came to give away his undergarment and his outer covering. At the cross his garments were taken away on earth, and on the day of Pentecost he anointed his church in the mantle of the Holy Spirit from heaven. Jesus gave away every covering that he had, in heaven and on earth.

Those called to wear the garment of God must also live a life of continual sacrifice. This entails giving away heavenly mantles as well as earthly possessions. Many people understand this and can sacrifice material possessions and give to the poor and needy. Unfortunately, lots of Christians will give to help missions that are deserving of charity, but never want to give up their own positions of power. They may give away their shirt, but never their cloak. It is a sad sight to observe someone so wrapped up in their own ministry that they have forgotten the call to sacrificial service. Instead of following the example of Jesus, who gave away the very spirit that clothed him,[256] many modern ministers claim

---

256      John 15:26

that they have a 'special anointing' of the Holy Spirit that belongs to them alone. They may let others touch it, but they have no intention of giving it to them. Jesus happily took off his clothes when dirty feet needed to be washed,[257] but many of his servants today would never let go of their position, or take off their official title, in order to perform the duties of a servant. Unfortunately, many insecure ministers hold their cloaks tightly to themselves, keeping their mantles under their sole control for their own benefit and promotion.

The genuine garment of God can always be given away. True ministers recognise and understand that freely they have received, so freely they can give away.[258] There is never any fear of loss, as when more is given away, even more will be provided. When the Holy Spirit clothes and anoints someone for ministry, he expects all of his gifts and covering to flow out to others. It is a garment of love and must never be held as a selfish personal possession.

---

257      John 13:4
258      Matt. 10:8

### *Garment of Love*

*Col. 3:12-14 'Clothe yourselves with compassion, kindness, humility, gentleness and patience...And over all these virtues put on love, which binds them all together in perfect unity.'*

When a Christian wears the garment of God they will exhibit the same character traits as Jesus. When the Holy Spirit clothes a believer, then their lives will produce the fruit of the Spirit as a result. Each aspect of the above mentioned virtues is always in evidence when God's garment is worn. If these characteristics are missing from a Christian's life, serious questions must be asked concerning whether the garment of the Holy Spirit is being worn at all.

Although many aspects of the garment of God have been discussed in this book, the most essential and profound component of Christ's clothing is also the simplest. The greatest aspect of the garment of God is love. Love is the material that binds all aspects of the garment together. Without love, the clothing will unravel. When Jesus came to earth, God clothed himself in Love. God loved the world and Jesus loved all those he met on earth. The Holy Spirit now clothes his church in the same love, so that they can love others and bid them to come and be robed in the garment of God.

Lightning Source UK Ltd.
Milton Keynes UK
UKOW05f0603260417
299914UK00003B/100/P

9 780995 738614